Integrative Acupressure[sm]

Acupressure Atlas

A Directory of the Points &

Meridians of Chinese Medicine

Specific to Hands-On Work

Sam McClellan

A Finger Press Book

A Finger Press Book
Published by Sam McClellan
8 River Drive, Hadley, MA 01035

First edition: September 2022
v8

Printed in the United States of America
ISBN: 9798846305427
Imprint: Independently published

Special thanks to Iona Teeguarden, the creator of Jin Shin Do acupressure and the training program which was my first experience of acupressure, and to Satya Ambrose, ND, LAc, who took the time and effort to introduce me to the deeper principles of acupuncture and Chinese medicine.

And to my lovely wife, Carrie, for her patience and support and everything else.

Contents

Integrative Acupressure Meridian Atlas

Introduction

I seldom read introductions so I'll make this short.

As a long-term acupressure practitioner, I've always longed for a book like this. Most books and charts of the Organ Meridians are designed for acupuncturists, who have no need for a clear description of the paths of the meridians between points. Hence, the meridian charts are simplified and don't show the true pathways of Qi. Being able to release along the entire length of a meridian ("running" the meridian) is one of the strengths of acupressure, hence having charts with accurate pathways can enhance our work.

In addition, since six of the eight the Extraordinary Meridians have no points of their own and include points from the twelve Organ Meridians, acupuncturists have no need for charts of them and so there are very few charts showing the paths of the Extra Meridians. Again, having accurate charts allows an acupressurist to release along the entire pathway.

Also the *cun*, the standard form of measurement used by acupuncturists, makes sense if you're trying to put a needle into a point but for acupressurists makes much less sense because once you find a point, you then need to take your hand off it so that you can put your finger on it. The finger measurement used in this book means that once you measure the distance, your finger is already on the point.

Lastly my previous book, *Integrative Acupressure: A Hands-on Guide to Balancing the Body's Structure and Energy for Health and Healing*, was in a smaller format so the charts I created were hard to read, and the point directory was in a separate part of the book which meant flipping back and forth between charts and points. I wanted to have all the relevant information related to the meridians in one place, in a large and easy to view format, and to be able to see the locations of the points that are being described on every page along with overall views of the meridians.

With this atlas, I finally have the book I've wanted. I hope you find it useful.

— *Sam McClellan*

A few relevant points (pardon the pun):

Note that I have chosen to capitalize any words that refer to anything specific to Chinese medicine, including ones that aren't normally capitalized like Yin and Yang, Meridian, and the names of the Organs to distinguish them from any Western terms. For example, when describing the Western view of the stomach versus the Chinese view of the Stomach.

Also, the information provided on this site is intended for your knowledge of Chinese medicine and the acupressure meridians and points only and is not a substitute for professional medical advice or treatment for a medical condition.

Lastly, you can keep track of my books, online and in-person trainings, music recordings including the Music of the Five Elements, and other related activities on my website https://integrativeacupressure.com, or https://sammcclellan.com will get you to the same place.

The Meridians of Acupressure

The twelve Organ Meridians and eight Extraordinary Meridians, or Extra Meridians, form the web of energy that weaves the various functions and structures of the body/mind together. They function both as the source of energy and the controllers of how that energy is used, circulate Qi throughout the body, activating, energizing, balancing and regulating all the functions of the body/mind.

We will be discussing the eight Extraordinary Meridians in chapter 14.

The Twelve Organ Meridians

While the Organ Meridians share the same name as organs in the body, they each include more than just that organ. For example, the Gall Bladder Meridian governs the gallbladder, that small sack tucked under the liver that contains and concentrates the bile produced by the liver and then squirts it out into the duodenum for digesting fats, but the Meridian is also associated with most of the head and the sides of the body. If the gallbladder is removed, the Gall Bladder Meridian keeps functioning. Think of it like the city of New York and the state of New York—they share the same name but one is only a small but important part of the other.

Each Organ Meridian is paired with a sibling Meridian, one Yin channel which corresponds to the solid organs of the body (Lung, Spleen, Heart, Liver and Kidney) and the other Yang corresponding to the hollow organs (Large Intestine, Stomach, Small Intestine, Gall Bladder and Bladder). The Yin Meridians govern more internal functions such as metabolism and circulation, the Yang Meridians govern more external functions such as the immune system and digestion.

While you may think of your digestive system as inside the body and therefore Yin, think of the body like a donut with the digestive system being the hole. The interior of the digestive system is effectively the outside of the body. When properly functioning, the digestive system determines what should be allowed into the body and what should be eliminated.

Each pair of Meridians is associated with one of the Five Elements - Wood, Fire, Earth, Metal and Water - and is associated with the qualities of that Element. For example, the Kidney and Bladder Meridians are associated with the Water element, which means they are also related to hearing, the salty taste, black or blue color, cold, the bones, and the hair on the head. A person with deficient

Water might crave salt, have hearing or ear difficulties, feel cold easily, have a black or blue hue to their skin, or have less hair on their head.

You might have noticed that I said twelve Organ Meridians, but I only listed ten Organs. The other two Meridians are the Pericardium Meridian and the Triple Warmer Meridian. The Pericardium Meridian is related to the pericardium, the protective sac which encloses the heart. The Pericardium Meridian is seen as an extension of the Heart Meridian and serves to protect the Heart both physically and emotionally. The Triple Warmer Meridian does not have a specific organ associated with it. It is concerned with balancing the overall functions of the body, including the endocrine system and overall metabolism. It works with the other Organ Meridians that are more specific to particular functions and structures.

Energy Circulation in the Meridians

The Organ Meridians are actually part of a larger flow of energy that circles through the entire body three times, with Qi in the Yin Meridians traveling inferiorly (with the arms up) and in the Yang Meridians traveling superiorly. The first cycle, including the paired Meridians of Lung/Large Intestine and Stomach/Spleen, moving from closer to the surface to deep within the body and back again. For the second cycle, including the paired Meridians of Heart/Small Intestine and Bladder/Kidney, moving from deeper to surface to deep. For the third cycle, including the paired Meridians of Pericardium/Triple Warmer and Gall Bladder/Liver, staying in the middle area between internal and external.

For the Yin Meridians, Tai is surface, Jue is transition, and Shao is deep and for the Yang Meridians, Tai is surface, Shao is middle, and Ming is deep. This is the path of energy in the Meridians starting with the Lung Meridian through the Liver Meridian and back to Lung.

First Cycle: Lung of Hand Tai Yin (external) - Large Intestine of Hand Yang Ming (internal) - Stomach of Foot Yang Ming (internal) - Spleen of Foot Tai Yin (external)

Second Cycle: Heart of Hand Shao Yin (internal) - Small Intestine of Hand Tai Yang (external) - Bladder of Foot Tai Yang (external) - Kidney of Foot Shao Yin (internal)

Third Cycle: Pericardium of Hand Jue Yin (middle) - Triple Warmer of Hand Shao Yang (middle) - Gall Bladder of Foot Shao Yang (middle) - Liver of Foot Jue Yin (hinge)

This larger flow of energy actually has a daily "tide" of high and low energy lasting for two hours in each Meridian. For example, from 3am to 5am is the high tide for Lung and the low tide for Bladder, and 5am to 7am is high tide for Large Intestine and low tide for Kidney.

Command Points

Each of the Organ Meridians have specific points which can be utilized to balance the Meridian (Source point), to balance it with its paired Meridian (Luo point), to increase or decrease the Meridian's activity (tonification/sedation points), to balance it in relation to other Meridians (Five Element point), to remedy acute issues (Accumulation point), and to balance the Meridian in its daily cycle (Horary point). The most commonly used command points are the Source and Lo points.

The command points are all distal to the elbows or knees on the peripheral limbs. The theory is that, like a wave approaching a beach gets larger because the water is getting shallower, the energy in the Meridians is the most changeable at the periphery because that is where it is closest to the surface and where it begins to change its energy as it transitions to the next Meridian.

Source Point

Also known as Yuan Points, this point is usually the most universally helpful point on the Meridian, it balances the energy in the Meridian and when used with other command points it increases the effect of other points unless that effect is not appropriate, in which case it acts to reduce or nullify the effect. Source points generate energy within the Organ Meridian, rather than moving energy between the Meridian and another Meridian.

Luo Point

Also known as the Junction point or Connecting point, this point sits where a branch Meridian goes between that Meridian and its Yin/Yang pair. It balances energy between a Meridian and its paired Meridian, sedating or tonifying the affected Meridian as needed. For example, if the Large Intestine pulse is excessive or otherwise showing signs of excess, you would sedate the Source point which is LI 4 along with activating (neither tonifying or sedating) the Lung Luo point or Lu 7. This is known as the guest-host method where the host source point of the affected Meridian is used with the guest, or paired Meridian's, Luo point.

Other command points include the following:

Five Element Point

Each Meridian has a point for each of the Five Elements. As I said, each pair of Meridians is associated with an element.

The Element point before the Meridian's Element in the Five Elements acts as a tonification point, it pulls energy from the previous Element through the Creative Cycle. So, for example, if there is deficient energy in the Lung Meridian, working on Lu 9 the Earth point will pull energy from Earth, the Spleen and Stomach Meridians.

The Element point after the Meridian's Element acts as a sedation point, it moves energy out of the Meridian into the next Meridians in the Five Elements. For the Lung Meridian, this would be Lu 5, the Water point.

The other two Element points work through the Destructive Cycle which acts like a seesaw, increasing one Element and decreasing an opposite Element. For example, working on Lu 11, the Wood point on the Lung Meridian, balances the energy between Wood (Liver and Gall Bladder Meridians) to Metal and the Lung Meridian. Similarly Lu 10, the Fire point, will balance energy between the Heart and Small Intestine Meridians and the Lung Meridian. These Destructive Cycle points are less frequently used in this way compared to the other Command Points.

Each of the Element points is related to the path of water to the sea - Well, Spring, Stream, River and Sea - starting from the fingers or toes and moving toward the elbows or knees.

For the Yin Meridians, the associations start with the Wood point (Well):

Wood - Well, Fire - Spring, Earth - Stream, Metal - River, Water - Sea

And for the Yang Meridians the associations start with the Metal point (Well):

Metal - Well, Water - Spring, Wood - Stream, Fire - River, Earth - Sea

Accumulation Point

Also known as the Accumulating Points or Xi Cleft Points - this point is where the Meridian's Qi and Blood accumulate. They are often at or near the joints of the body. They are used primarily for acute conditions, especially pain, that involve their related organs/channels but can also be used for acute bleeding issues such as nosebleeds, coughing up blood and severe menstrual pain. You can think of them as points where energy accumulates because it can't get through farther on, and releasing this point will release the blockage. They are typically tender to the touch when there is an appropriate issue needing their release. The point should be dispersed (a gentle spreading movement rather than deep, pointed pressure). All but two of the Extra Meridians have accumulation points, the exceptions being the Penetrating and Belt Channels.

Horary Point

This is a time-based point which is used for increasing energy in a deficient Meridian. The Horary point works only during the peak time for that Meridian according to the energy circulation in the Meridians clock. For example, the Lung Meridian reaches its peak energy between 3am and 5am.

Stimulating the Horary point during this time will help fortify the Meridian and balance its functioning especially in relation to its circadian rhythm which can be thrown off by jet lag, change of seasons, or illness. Note that the Horary point is always the Element point of that particular Meridian, in the Five Element Points.

Other Point Sets

These are other point sets which can be used for determining issues and working to remedy them.

Shu Points - these are points on the back along the inner Bladder Meridian closer to the spine, each of which corresponds to a particular Organ or other structures including the diaphragm, upper and lower lumbar areas, the sacrum and the anal sphincter. They are typically used to treat more long-term (chronic) issues but can also become irritated and sore with acute issues.

Alarm (Bo) Points - The Alarm points are located on the front of the torso on several Meridians. The Alarm points are often used to determine acute or excessive issues with an organ.

Auricular Points - The points on the ears can be used to treat all areas of the body.

Point Location - Measuring Distance With Your Fingertips

The standard measurement in acupuncture is called the cun (pronounced 'soon' with a shortened 'oo'). A cun is measured as the width of the thumb at the first joint, although it is a relative measurement and varies according to the individual. So a child's cun would be significantly smaller, and the cun would be larger if you are working with a person with a larger belly or shorter legs.

For expediency and ease for beginners, I have adopted a "fingers" method for measurement—more appropriate for acupressure because when measuring cun, you are partially covering the point making it hard to get your finger in there. The fingers method measures the distance between the center of each fingertip, where you place your finger on the point or location, so your finger is perfectly placed on the point. Typically you would place your index finger on the point or location you are measuring from, then place your fingertips together in a line with the appropriate finger on the location we are measuring the total number of fingers from one location to another.

For example, if your index finger is on Lu 2 and your ring finger is on Lu 1, you would count that as 3 fingers. As mentioned above, this is relative to the size of the person you are working with along with their anatomical uniqueness.

The other possibility you'll see for locating points is that you will place your index finger at the edge of an anatomical location–against the side of a bone, for example.

As with the cun, the fingers measurement method is based on the person's fingers and needs to take into account differences in anatomy.

With practice, you will get an intuitive feel for distances. In addition, most acu points are in notable locations such as a small indentation, the center of a crease, the outside of a fingernail, or where the shaft of a bone meets the head.

For your information, and as a way of translating (bearing in mind the relativity of both the fingers and the cun method), two fingers' distance is equal to about 1 cun and four fingers' distance is equal to about 2 cun.

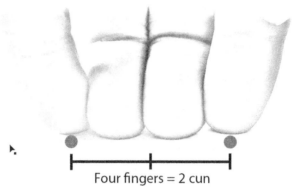

Four fingers = 2 cun

Glossary of Anatomical Terms

We use the following anatomical terms in the locations below. These are based on the Chinese anatomical position, where the toes are pointed ahead, the arms are up and the palms are facing forward as depicted in most of the charts.

Anterior, anteriorly - the front of the body, moving toward the front of the body.

Posterior, posteriorly - the back of the body, moving toward the back of the body.

Superior, superiorly - the upper area of the body or a body part, moving toward the upper body or a body part.

Inferior, inferiorly - the lower area of the body or a body part, moving toward the lower body or a body part.

Medial, medially - closer to the median line of the body (a line extending along the spine or center of the torso), movement toward the median line of the body

Lateral, laterally - farther from the median line of the body (a line extending along the spine or center of the torso), movement away from the median line of the body

Proximal, proximally - closer to the center of the body (the stomach area), movement toward the center of the body

Distal, distally - closer to the periphery of the body (hands, feet, head), movement toward the periphery of the body

手太陰肺經
Lung Meridian
of Hand Tai Yin (Greater Yin)

Primary Balancing and Five Element Points

Wood	Lu 11	Well
Fire	Lu 10	Spring
Source/Earth/Tonification	Lu 9	Stream
Metal/Horary	Lu 8	River
Water/Sedation	Lu 5	Sea
Luo	Lu 7	
Accumulation/Xi Cleft	Lu 6	

Key Attributes of the Lung Meridian

Element: Metal
Season: Autumn
Stage of Life: Harvest
Climate: Dryness
Sense Organ: Nose
Tissue Governed: Skin

Emotions: Grief/Sadness
Balanced Attributes: Integrity, Boundaries
Yang Organ: Large Intestine
Time: 3-5 am
Color: White
Flavor: Pungent/Acrid

Common Physical Symptoms of Imbalance:

Asthma
Bronchitis
Pneumonia
Chest Congestion
Claustrophobia
Coughing
Difficult Breathing

Excessive Mucus (Also Spleen)
Restlessness
Throat Sore
Voice Loss
Perspiration Deficient Or Excessive
Chest Collapsed Or Hollow

Common Emotional Symptoms of Imbalance:

Chronic or Long-term Grief, Sorrow
Compulsive Behaviors

Letting Go Too Much
Lack of Boundaries

About the Lung Meridian

The Lung Meridian governs the lungs and upper respiratory system, including the nose and sinuses, and controls the skin. It is paired with the Large Intestine Meridian.

The lungs are the primary organs of respiration, supplying the body with oxygen – essential for energy and life. We have two lungs, weighing together about two and a half pounds. They are located inside the rib cage, extending from slightly below the bottom of the sternum to just below the first rib. The lungs are composed of a thick mesh of capillaries whose purpose is to pass oxygen into blood cells.

In Chinese medicine, the Lungs receive Qi from the air, mix it with food, and disburse it throughout the body. How deeply we breathe shapes the Qi and gives it definition–a nervous, shallow breather will experience the same erratic energy and will tend to exhibit a nervous, insecure personality. Conversely, a deep, rhythmic breather will tend to have more vitality.

The Lung Meridian is paired with the Large Intestine Meridian, it flows into the Large Intestine Meridian. Problems affecting one affect the other. When the lungs are irritated by toxins, excess mucus is produced in all the mucus membranes, including the intestines. Consequently, in Chinese medicine, lung issues are often treated by working with the Large Intestine Meridian.

The emotions associated with the Lung and Large Intestine meridians are grief and sorrow, and the quality of acceptance and letting go. In excess, we see excessive acceptance, the "everything's okay with me" syndrome. In deficiency, we see lack of acceptance, stubbornness, and denial.

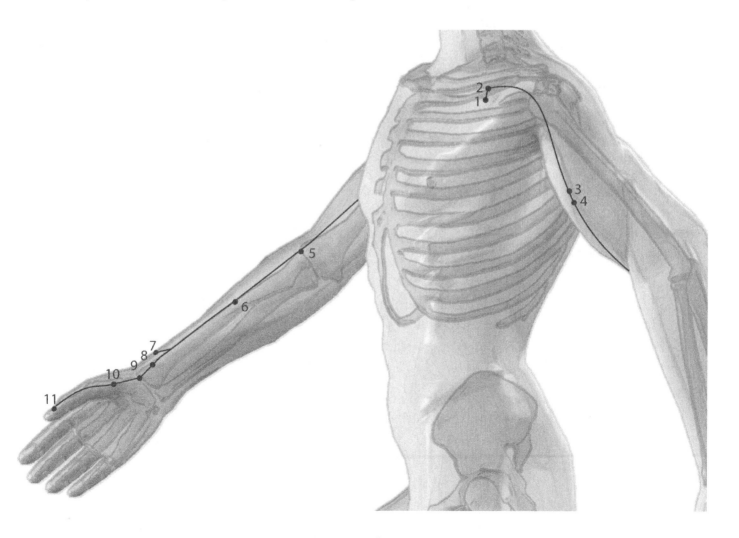

Lung Meridian Point Index

Lu 1 中府 Zhongfu "Middle Assembly" - Alarm Point, Entry Point
Follow the crease where the arm meets chest superiorly to just inferior to the clavicle, then 3 fingers medially just below clavicle to Lu 2, 3 fingers inferiorly to Lu 1.

Anxiety, Asthma, Bronchitis, Breathing Difficult, Tropical Fever, Heart Trouble, Chest or Muscular Rheumatism, Pleurisy, Shoulder Pain, Skin Problems, Tonsillitis, Trachea Problems, Tuberculosis.

Lu 2 雲門 Yunmen "Cloud Gate"
Follow the crease where the arm meets the chest up to just inferior to the clavicle, then 3 fingers medially.

Asthma, Breathing Difficult, Cough, Heart Problems, Tonsillitis.

Lu 3 天府 Tianfu "Upper Arm Assembly"
At the distal attachment of the deltoid muscle where it forms a "V", move anteriorly onto the belly of the biceps between the muscle fibers, then 2 fingers proximally toward the shoulder.

Arthritis (Fingers), Bronchitis, Cerebral Congestion, Coughing Blood, Depression, Fever, Headache, Nosebleed, Poisoning (Gas), Psychopathy, Vertigo (Dizzy), Vomiting.

Lu 4 俠白 Xiabai "Supporting the Lung"
3 fingers distally from Lu 3, or 7 fingers proximally from the crease of the elbow in the belly of the biceps between the muscle fibers.

Anxiety, Heart Problems, Vomiting (Dry Heaves).

Lu 5 尺澤 Chize "Cubit Marsh" - Sedation point, Water point, Sea point
On the interior of the elbow joint on the distal (thumb) side, two fingers laterally from the center of the joint.

Bronchitis, Difficulty Breathing, Chest Infection, Coughing Blood, Facial Paralysis, Nervous Disorders, Paralysis, Pleurisy, Stroke, Tuberculosis.

Lu 6 孔最 Kongzui "Collection Hole" Accumulation point
6 fingers distally from the elbow (Lu5) toward the wrist.

Alcoholism, Cough, Coughing Blood, Hoarse, Headache, Hemorrhoids, Nasal Inflammation, Nervous Disorders, Sweatless Fever, Tonsillitis.

Lu 7 列缺 Lieque "Interrupted Sequence" - Luo point
3 fingers proximally toward the elbow from Lu 9, on the thumb side of the tendon in the niche where the shaft of the radius expands into the head.

Difficulty Breathing, Facial Paralysis, Headache (Migraine), Lateral Paralysis, Neck Pain, Toothache, Tuberculosis, Water Retention.

Lu 8 經渠 Jingqu "Channel Ditch" - Metal point, Horary point, River point
2 fingers proximally toward the elbow from Lu 9, on the point of the head of the radius.

Asthenia (Weakness), Cough, Esophagus Problems, Nasal Inflammation, Paralysis, Tonsillitis, Vomiting.

Lu 9 太淵 Taiyuan "Great Deep Pool" - Source point, Earth point, Tonification point

In the niche at the crease of the wrist between the head of the radius and the carpal bones (trapezium), laterally toward the thumb side of the tendon.

Conjunctivitis, Coughing Blood, Cornea Inflammation, Emphysema, Insomnia.

Lu 10 魚際 Yuji "Fish Border" - Fire point, Spring point

4 fingers distally from Lu 9 in the belly of the thenar eminence (meaty thumb muscle), or halfway between the base knuckle and Lu 9, then one finger medially toward the pinky side.

Anxiety, Headache, Insomnia, Tonsillitis, Vertigo.

Lu 11 少商 Shaoshang "Lesser Metal" - Wood point, Well point

Base of the nail on the lateral (thumb) side.

Cerebral Congestion, Pulmonary Congestion, Fear, Insomnia, Meningitis, Mumps & Swollen Glands, Stroke, Tonsillitis.

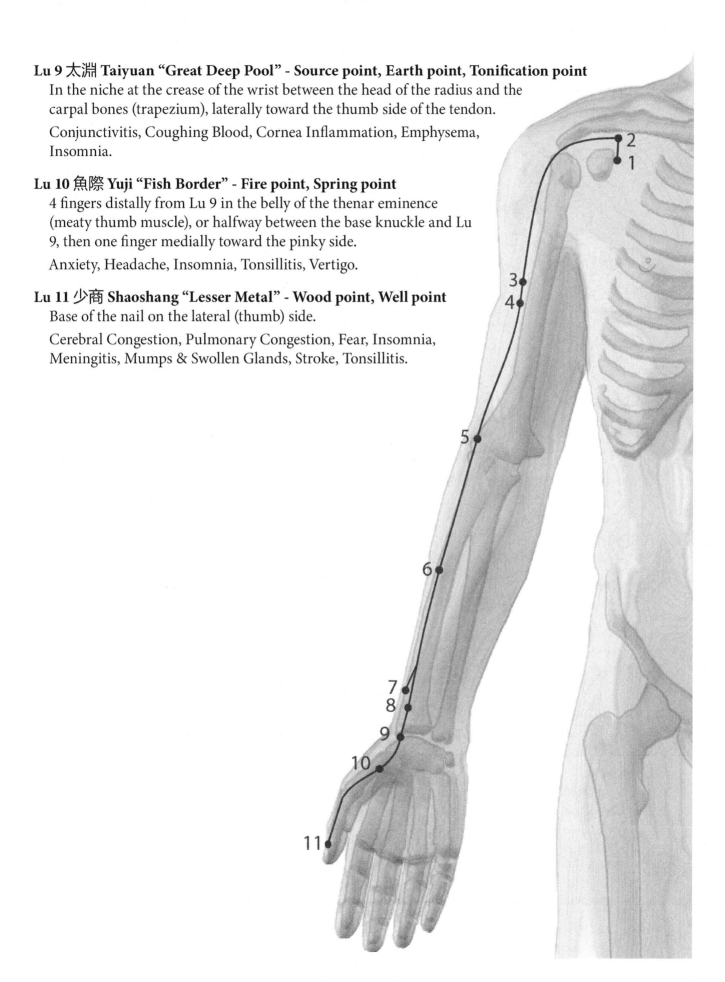

手陽明大腸經
Large Intestine Meridian
of Hand Yang Ming (Bright Yang)

Primary Balancing and Five Element Points

Metal/Horary	LI 1	Well
Water/Sedation	LI 2	Spring
Wood	LI 3	Stream
Fire	LI 5	River
Earth/Tonification	LI 11	Sea
Source	LI 4	
Luo	LI 6	
Accumulation/Xi Cleft	LI 7	

Key Attributes of the Large Intestine Meridian

Element: Metal
Season: Autumn
Stage of Life: Harvest
Climate: Dryness
Sense Organ: Nose
Tissue Governed: Skin

Emotions: Grief, Sadness
Balanced Attributes: Integrity/Boundaries
Yin Organ: Lung
Time: 5-7 am
Color: White
Flavor: Pungent/Acrid

Common Physical Symptoms of Imbalance:

Constipation
Intestinal Cramping
Diarrhea (Also Spleen, Kidney, Liver)
Headache (Also Liver, Gall Bladder)
Shoulder pain

Nasal congestion, runny nose
Nosebleeds
Toothache
Throat Sore
Lung Symptoms

Common Emotional Symptoms of Imbalance:

Excessive worry
Chronic grief, sadness

Compulsive attention to detail
Stubbornness

About the Large Intestine Meridian

The Large Intestine meridian governs the large intestines (colon) which is approximately two inches in diameter and six feet long, starting in the lower right abdomen and going up to just under the right rib cage (ascending colon), then crossing to the left side (transverse colon) then descending to the lower left abdomen (descending colon) and across to just behind the pubic bone (sigmoid colon) where it becomes the rectum and ending at the anus.

The primary function of the large intestine organ, according to Western medicine, is to receive waste from the small intestine, remove any excess water and nutrients from the feces, and produce vitamin K and various B vitamins, ultimately eliminating food waste from the body.

The Large Intestine meridian is paired with the Lung meridian which passes the Qi on to it. Problems affecting one affect the other. When the lungs are irritated by toxins, excess mucus is produced in all the mucus membranes, including the intestines. Consequently, in Chinese medicine, large intestine issues are often treated by working with the Lung meridian.

The emotions associated with the Lung and Large Intestine meridians are grief and sorrow, and the quality of acceptance and letting go. In excess, we see excessive acceptance, the "everything's okay with me" syndrome. In deficiency, we see lack of acceptance, stubbornness, and denial.

Large Intestine Meridian Point Index

LI 1 商陽 Shangyang "Metal Yang" - Horary point

At the lateral (thumb) side of the base of the nail of the index finger.

Boils on Face, Breathing Problems, Cerebral Congestion, Chest Congestion, Deafness, Ears Ring, Fever, Jaundice, Laryngitis, Shock, Stroke, Sweat Absent, Swollen Jaw, Tonsillitis, Toothache.

LI 2 二間 Erjian "Second Point" - Sedation point, Water point

Just distal to the third (base) knuckle, where the shaft meets the edge of the knuckle, at the juncture of the top meets the side of the finger.

Constipation, Esophagus Problems, Laryngitis, Nosebleed, Shoulder Pain, Tonsillitis, Toothache.

LI 3 三間 Sanjian "Third Point" - Wood point

Just proximal to the base knuckle where the shaft meets the knuckle, at the juncture of the top and side of the finger.

Abdominal Inflammation, Boils on Face, Diarrhea, Eyelid Pain or Itch, Flatulence, Headache, Chapped Lips, Lockjaw, Dry Mouth, Salivation Excessive, Shoulder Pain, Tongue Inflammation, Toothache.

LI 4 合谷 He Gu Junction Valley" - Source point

The common acupuncture location is midway distally in the soft area between the thumb and the index finger. In Integrative Acupressure, it's located on the lateral edge of the index metacarpal where the shaft meets the proximal knuckle.

Deafness, Depression, Digestion, Facial Problems, Headache, Insomnia, Mental Disorders, Migraine, Mouth Problems, Night Sweats, Nosebleed, Pain Control, Period Arrested, Revival (Shock), Tonsillitis, Toothache, Vision Problems.

LI 5 陽谿 Yangxi "Yang Stream" - Fire point

In the crease of the wrist between the two large thumb tendons in the depression formed when the thumb is extended out and back.

Deafness, Ears Ring, Headache, Mental Disorders, Sensory Paralysis, Tonsillitis, Toothache.

LI 6 偏歷 Pianli "Diverging Passage" - Luo Point

Start from LI 5, go 6 fingers proximally on the edge of the top of the radius.

Breathing Problems, Deafness, Ears Ring, Nosebleed, Paralysis (One Side), Throat Dry, Toothache.

LI 7 溫溜 Wenliu "Warm Flow" - Accumulation Point

Starting from LI 5, located 3 fingers proximally.

Canker or Cold Sore, Eczema, Flatulence, Mouth Tumor, Swollen Glands, Throat Sore, Tongue Inflammation, Tonsillitis.

LI 8, 9, 10 - all located 2 fingers from each other.

LI 8 下廉 Xialian "Lower Point at the Border"

4 fingers proximally from LI 7, or from LI 11 distally 3 fingers to LI 10, 3 more fingers to LI 8.

Breast Inflammation or Tumor, Bladder Paralysis, Low Chest Pain, Flatulence, Pulmonary Tuberculosis, Tuberculosis.

LI 9 上廉 Shanglian "Upper Point at the Border"

Find LI 11, move distally 3 fingers to LI 10, then 2 fingers to LI 9.

Bladder Paralysis, Flatulence, Lateral Paralysis, Mental Fatigue, Mucous Discharge, Stroke.

LI 10 手三里 Shousanli "Arm Three Miles"

Find LI 11, move distally 3 fingers to LI 10. WIth your index finger on LI 10, your middle finger will be on LI 9 and ring finger will be on LI 8.

Arm Neuralgia, Chills, Lateral Paralysis, Stroke, Swollen Glands, Toothache, Tuberculosis.

LI 11 曲池 Quchi "Pool at the Bend" - Tonification point, Earth point

Hold your arm as if it were in a sling, then follow across on the superior line of the forearm (along the radius) proximally toward the elbow until you reach the elbow (humerus) just anterior to the biceps tendon. The point is located distally 3 fingers and pressing into the radius bone

Anemia, Pressure on Brain, Chest Infection, Constipation, Depression, Headache, Intercostal Neuralgia, Lateral Paralysis, Scapula Pain, Shoulder Pain, Skin Problems, Tonsillitis, Toothache.

LI 12 肘髎 Zhouliao "Elbow Bone Hole"

From LI 11, on a diagonal laterally and proximally, measure 3 fingers onto the head of the humerus.

Arm Neuralgia, Lateral Paralysis, Shoulder Pain.

LI 13 手五里 Shouwuli "Arm Five Miles"

From LI 12, measure 4 fingers proximally and press into the humerus bone.

Arm Neuralgia, Cough, Fright, Lymph Gland Diseases, Pneumonia, Rheumatism, Scrofula, Sleep Excessive.

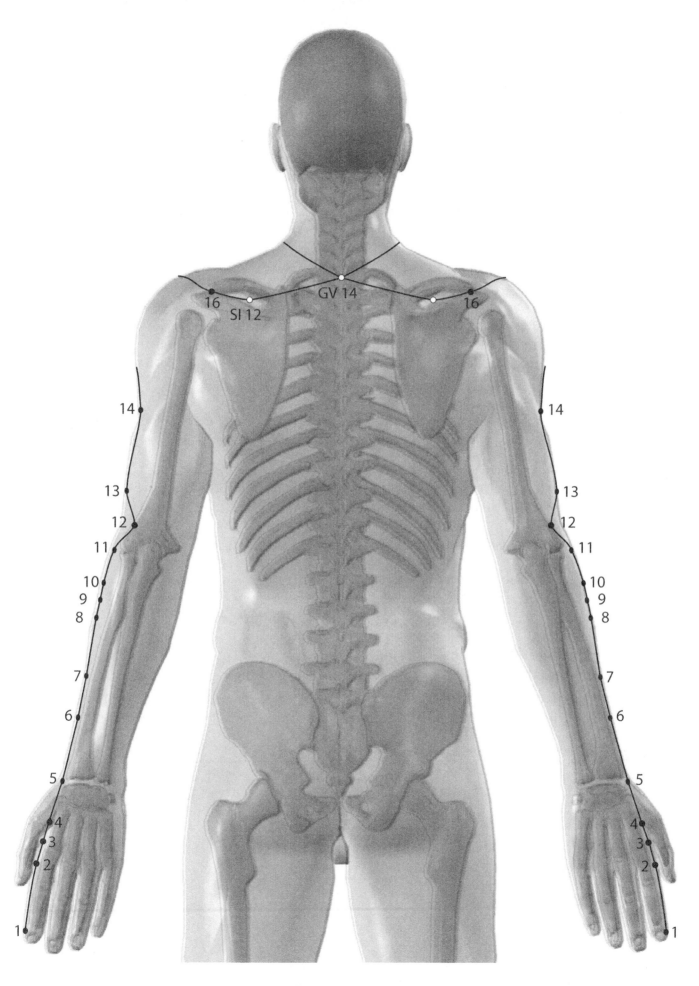

Large Intestine Meridian

LI 14 臂臑 Binao "Upper Arm"

From the lateral middle area of the upper arm, grasp the inner and outer sides of the deltoid muscle and follow them distally to where they come together and attach to the humerus, forming the bottom of a V. LI 14 is 2 fingers to the anterior of the attachment point of the V pressing into the humerus.

Arm Neuralgia, Arthritis, Headache, Scrofula, Sore Throat.

LI 15 肩髃 Jianyu "Shoulder and Clavicle"

Measure 3 fingers medially from the lateral end of the clavicle, LI 15 is on the underside of the clavicle where the shaft and the head meet, in a niche.

Arm Neuralgia, Arthritis, Hypertension, Lateral Paralysis.

LI 16 巨骨 Jugu "Large Bone"

Follow along the top of the spine of the scapula (the bony ridge stretching across the scapula). Move laterally towards the shoulder as far as you can go and still be in the soft area between the scapula and the clavicle where they form a V. Press into the flesh there.

Arm Pain or Paralysis, Fear or Restlessness in Children, Vomiting Blood

The meridian continues over the shoulder through SI 12 and goes out to meet the spine at GV 14 between T2 and T3, and then goes forward to the front of the neck.

LI 17 天鼎 Tianding "Head's Tripod"

Find the medial tip (horn) of the clavicle and measure 3 fingers laterally along the superior aspect of the clavicle, then 3 fingers superiorly from there. You will be posterior to the sternocleidomastoid (SCM) muscle.

Angina Pectoralis, Nasal Inflammation, Any Throat Problems, Tonsillitis.

LI 18 扶突 Futu "Beside the Prominence"

Measure 3 fingers up from 17 along the back of the sternocleidomastoid muscle (SCM).

Asthma, Breathing Problems, Cough, Laryngitis, Nosebleeds.

LI 19 口禾髎 Kouheliao "Mouth Grain Hole"

At the bottom of the outside of the nose in the depression pressing slightly inferiorly.

Facial Paralysis or Spasms, Lockjaw, Mucous Excessive, Nasal Polyps or Ulcers, Loss of Smell, Shock, Swollen Glands, Tears Excess or Deficient.

LI 20 迎香 Yingxiang "Receiving Fragrance"

A tight 2 fingers superiorly from LI 19 in the depression pressing slightly superiorly.

Breathing Problems, Facial Paralysis, Swollen Glands, Nasal Polyps or Ulcers, Nosebleed, Respiratory Inflammation, Loss of Smell.

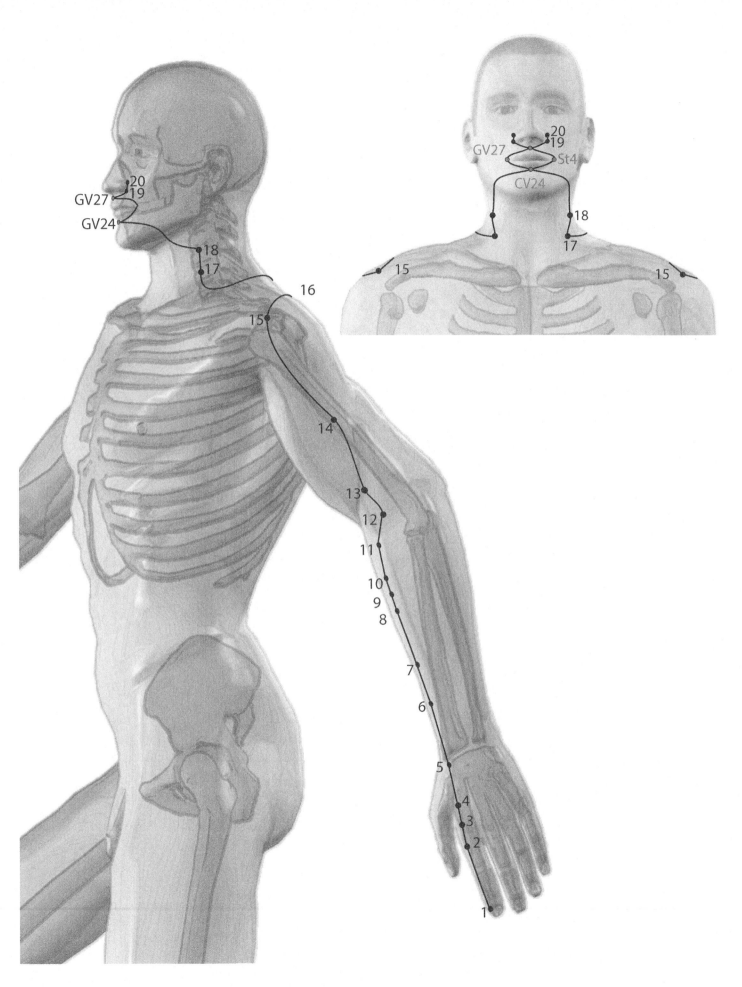

Large Intestine Meridian

足陽明胃經
Stomach Meridian

of Foot Yang Ming (Bright Yang)

Primary Balancing and Five Element Points

Metal	St 45	Well
Water/Sedation	St 44	Spring
Wood	St 43	Stream
Fire/Tonification	St 41	River
Earth/Horary	St 36	Sea
Source	St 42	
Luo	St 40	
Accumulation/Xi Cleft	St 34	

Key Attributes of the Stomach Meridian

Element: Earth	Emotions: Worry, Obsession
Season: Late Summer	Balanced Attributes: Bonding, Clarity
Stage of Life: Harvest	Yin Organ: Spleen
Climate: Wet	Time: 7-9 am
Sense Organ: Taste	Color: Yellow
Tissue Governed: Muscles, Lymph	Flavor: Sweet

Common Physical Symptoms of Imbalance:

Abdomen (Upper) Distention	Neck, Throat Swollen
Groaning	Vomiting
Yawning	Abdomen Swollen, Full
Jaw Tension	Stomach Area Cold
Knee Pain, Swelling	Frequent Hunger, Thirst
Lip, Mouth Sores	Sleepy After Eating
Mouth Sideways, Crooked	Abdominal Pain

Common Emotional Symptoms of Imbalance:

Anxiety, chronic nervousness tension   Inability to feel emotionally stable, centered
Critical
Lack of understanding, compassion

About the Stomach Meridian

Shaped like a boxing glove, the stomach is a muscular sac joined to the esophagus at the top and to the small intestine at the bottom. Western medicine holds that the stomach has five functions: storing food; making digestive juices; churning the food into an homogenous mix called chyme; digesting proteins from foods; and releasing the treated food into the small intestine.

The Stomach and Spleen are regarded as paired organs, in Chinese medicine they are considered the Earth Element in the Five Element System. Together, the Stomach and Spleen control digestion by dispersing Qi throughout the digestive tract.

Since the stomach meridian begins at the mouth, it is said to control the mouth, tongue, and esophagus. Thus, it nourishes and controls the preparation of food for digestion.

One notable difference between the Western and Eastern views of the stomach is that in Chinese medicine, which is more concerned with function than structure, the duodenum is considered to be part of the stomach, whereas in Western physiology the duodenum is considered to be the first part of the small intestine. Functionally, the duodenum is where the pancreas and liver both secrete their digestive juices; it is an area, therefore, more related to preparation of food than to assimilation, similarly to the stomach.

The emotions associated with the Spleen and Stomach meridians are related to bonding - in excess, there is an inability to separate—from others, from possessions, from feelings especially negative feelings. In deficiency, there is a lack of the ability to bond and to have compassion or empathy.

Stomach Meridian Point Index

St 1 承泣 Chengqi "Tears Container"
Directly below the pupil on the flat of the bone.

Cornea Inflammation, Eyelid Spasm, Tears Excessive, Night Blindness.

St 2 四白 Sibai "Four Directions Brightness"
2 fingers inferior to St 1.

Facial Abscess, Dizzy, Headache, Eye Problems, Nasal Mucous.

St 3 巨髎 Juliao "Large Bone Hole"
Directly inferior to St 2 at the level of the base of nose, just inferior and slightly medial to the inside edge of the cheekbone.

Facial Abscess, Lip Problems, Myopia, Tears Excessive, Vision & Eye Problems.

St 4 地倉 Dicang "Earth Granary"
At the corner of the lips.

Eye Muscle Problems, Muteness, Myopia.

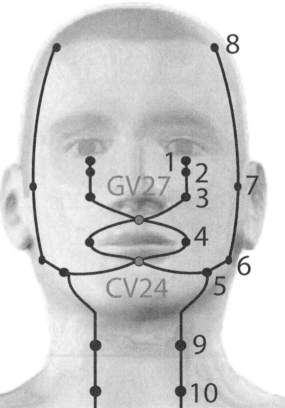

St 5 大迎 Daying "Large Receptacle" (Facial Artery)

From the posterior angle of the jaw, anteriorly 5 fingers on the lower jaw, anterior to the masseter muscle.

Eye Muscle Problems, Lockjaw, Swollen Glands.

St 6 頰車 Jiache "Jaw Bone"

From the posterior angle of the jaw, move superiorly 2 fingers and anteriorly 2 fingers in the belly of the masseter muscle.

Teeth Grinding, Hoarseness, Laryngitis, Neck Pain or Problems, Nervous Exhaustion.

St 7 下關 Xiaguan "Below the Arch"

3 fingers anterior to the ear, just below the zygomatic arch in the niche.

Deafness, Dizzy, Weakness.

St 8 頭維 Touwei "Head's Corner"

On the hairline corner, 4 fingers laterally from the corner of the eye and superiorly 6 fingers.

Cerebral Congestion, Conjunctivitis, Migraine, Vision Problems.

St 9 人迎 Renying "Man'sPrognosis" (Carotid Artery)

At the pulse point on the neck, where the neck, esophagus and underside of chin meet.

Asthma, Breathing Problems, Bronchitis, Chest Fullness, Coughing, Hypertension, Neck & Throat Problems, Thyroid, Tonsils, Voice Problems, Vomiting.

St 10 水突 Shuitu "Liquid Passage"

Halfway between St 9 and ST 11, on part of the thyroid gland.

Breathing Problems, Bronchitis, Nasal Inflammation, Whooping Cough.

St 11 氣舍 Qishe "Residence of Breath Qi"

On the superior aspect of the clavicle pressing inferiorly, 2 fingers laterally from the sharp point of the medial head of the clavicle, where the shaft meets the head.

Breathing Problems, Bronchitis, Nasal Inflammation, Whooping Cough.

St 12 缺盆 Quepen "Empty Basin"

3 fingers laterally from St 11 on the superior aspect of the clavicle, or 4 fingers laterally from the medial head of the clavicle.

Breathing Problems, Pleurisy, Scrofula.

St 13 氣戶 Qihu "Door of Breath"

On the inferior aspect of the clavicle directly inferior to St 12.

Resuscitation, Bronchitis, Cough, Diaphragm Spasm, Hiccups, Pulmonary Congestion.

St 14 庫房 Kufang "Breath Storeroom"

3 fingers inferior to St 13, between the 1st and 2nd ribs - 1st intercostal space.

Resuscitation, Bronchitis, Pulmonary Congestion.

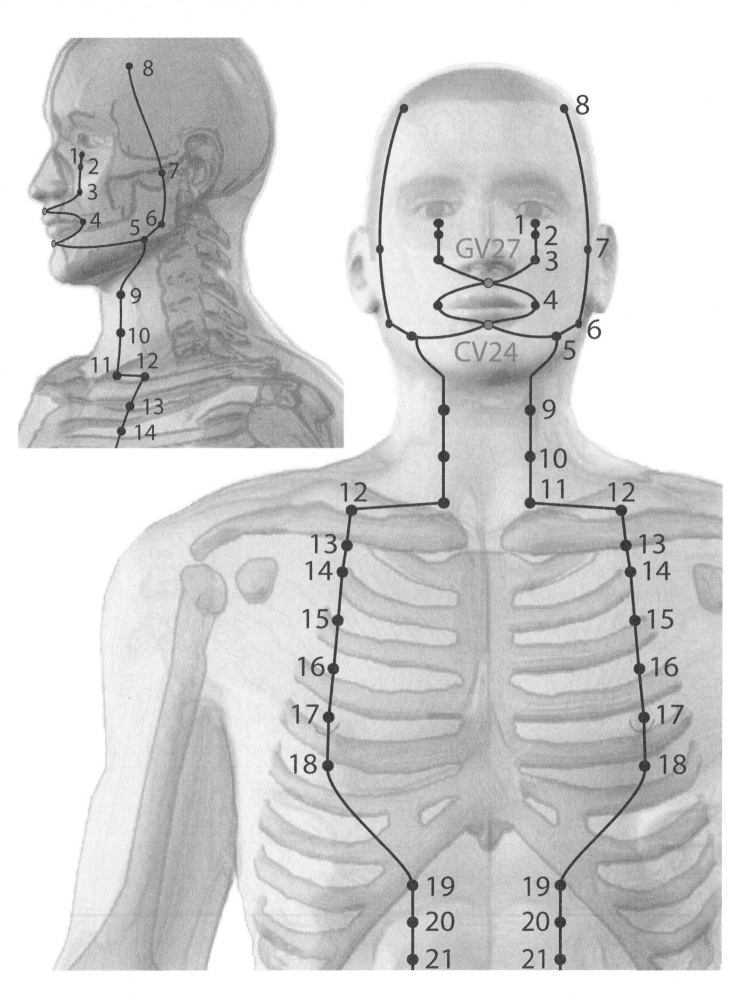

Stomach Meridian

St 15 - 18 are evenly spaced in the intercostal (between the ribs) spaces moving inferiorly toward and just below the nipple on men. For women on the breast, the points are evenly spaced to and past the nipple.

St 15 屋翳 Wuyi "Hiding the Breath"

3 fingers inferior to St 14, between the 2nd and 3rd ribs - 2nd intercostal space.

Coughing, Edema, Paralysis, Vomiting Blood.

St 16 膺窗 Yingchuang "Breast Window"

3 fingers inferior to St 15, between the 3rd and 4th ribs - 3nd intercostal space.

Breast Tumor, Emphysema, Flatulence, Pulmonary Congestion.

St 17 乳中 Ruzhong "Breast Centre (Nipple)"

On the nipple, between the 4th and 5th ribs.

Coughing.

St 18 乳根 Rugen "Breast Root"

3 fingers below the nipple, between the 5th and 6th ribs.

Breast Inflammation, Coughing, Milk Insufficient, Pleurisy.

St 19 不容 Burong "Not Contained"

5 fingers diagonally inferior and medial to St 18. Measure 4 fingers laterally from the midline to the level where you are on the edge of the rib cage.

Anorexia, Breathing Difficult, Cough, Vomiting.

St 20 承满 Chengman "Receiving Fullness"

2 fingers inferior to St 19.

Anorexia, Abdomen Swollen, Cough, Diarrhea, Flatulence, Jaundice, Vomiting Blood.

St 21 梁門 Liangmen "Beam Gate"

2 fingers inferior to St 20, 4 fingers superior to St 25.

Anorexia, Indigestion, Mouth Inflammation.

St 22 關門 Guanmen "Shutting the Gate"

2 fingers inferior to St 21, 3 fingers superior to St 25

Anorexia, Constipation, Edema, Hernia, Indigestion, Intestinal Mucous, Mouth Inflamed, Urinary Incontinence.

St 23 太乙 Taiyi "Great Unity"

2 fingers inferior to St 22, 2 fingers superior to St 25

Anorexia, Dementia, Hernia, Indigestion, Mouth Inflamed.

St 24 滑肉門 Huaroumen "Chime Gate"

2 fingers inferior to St 23, 2 fingers superior to St 25

All Stomach Problems, Dysmenorrhea, Edema, Epilepsy, Kidney Inflammation, Psychopathy, Womb Inflammation.

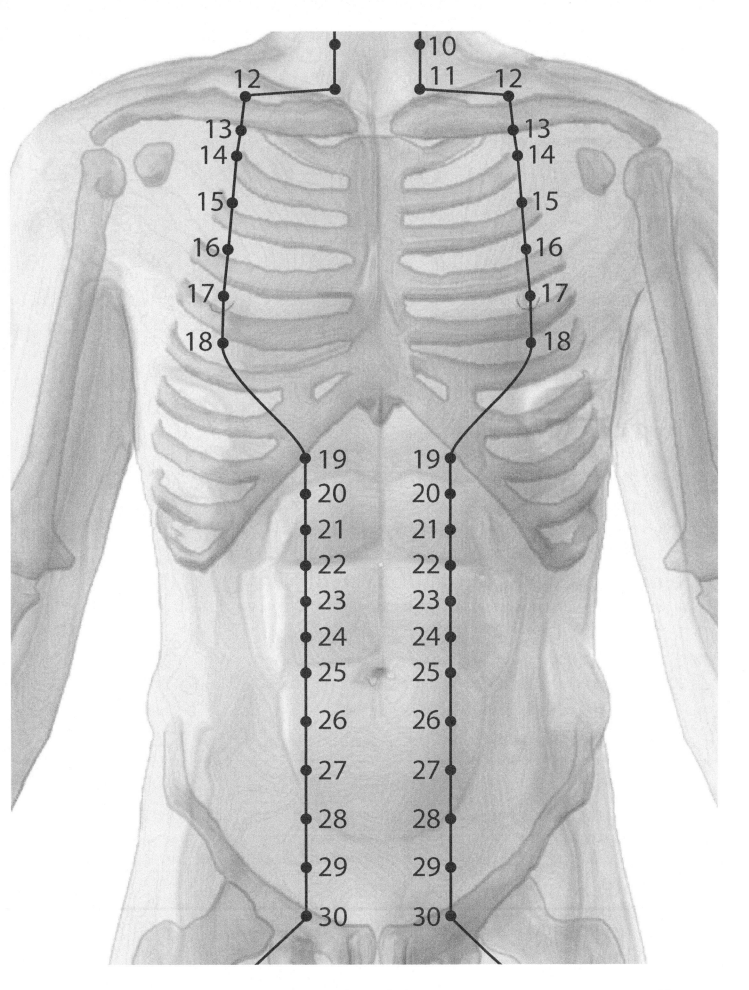

Stomach Meridian

St 25 天樞 Tianshu "Heavenly Pivot"

5 fingers laterally from the navel.

All Stomach Problems, Appendicitis, Diarrhea, Dysmenorrhea, Fever Intermittent, Kidney Inflammation, Womb Inflammation.

St 26 外陵 Wailing "Outer Mound"

3 fingers inferior to St 25.

Intestinal Spasm.

St 27-29 are evenly spaced, around 3 fingers from the previous point. St 29 is 2 fingers superior to St 30.

St 27 大巨 Daju "Great Bulge"

3 fingers inferior to St 26.

Constipation, Hernia, Insomnia, Urinary Suppression.

St 28 水道 Shuidao "Waterway"

3 fingers inferior to St 27.

Bone Marrow Inflammation, Kidney & Genital Inflammation, Urinary Suppression.

St 29 歸來 (归来) Guilai "Restoring Position"

3 fingers inferior to St 28.

Amenorrhea, All Genital Problems, Vaginal Discharge.

St 30 氣沖 Qichong "Qi Surge"

Just superior to the outside corner of the pubic bone.

Abdominal Pain, All Genital Problems, Hernia, Impotency, Lumbago.

St 31 髀關 Biguan "Thigh Gate"

From St 30, 6 fingers inferiorly and 7 fingers laterally, slightly lateral to the shaft of the femur.

Swollen Glands (Groin).

St 32 伏兔 Futu "Crouching Rabbit"

6 fingers superior to St 33, slightly lateral to the shaft of the femur.

Headache, Knees Cold, Uterine or Ovarian Problems.

St 33 阴市 Yinshi "Yin Market"

2 fingers superior to St 34.

Colic, Diabetes, Parkinson's Disease, Uterine Spasm.

St 34 梁丘 Liangqiu "Ridge Mound"

3 fingers superior to the superior medial corner of the patella.

Acute Gastric Pain, Acute Mastitis, Knee Swelling and Pain, Lower Extremities Paralysis or Weakness.

St 35 犊鼻 Dubi "Calf's Nose"

2 fingers lateral to the inferior lateral corner of the patella in the depression.

Arthritis.

Integrative Acupressure Meridian Atlas

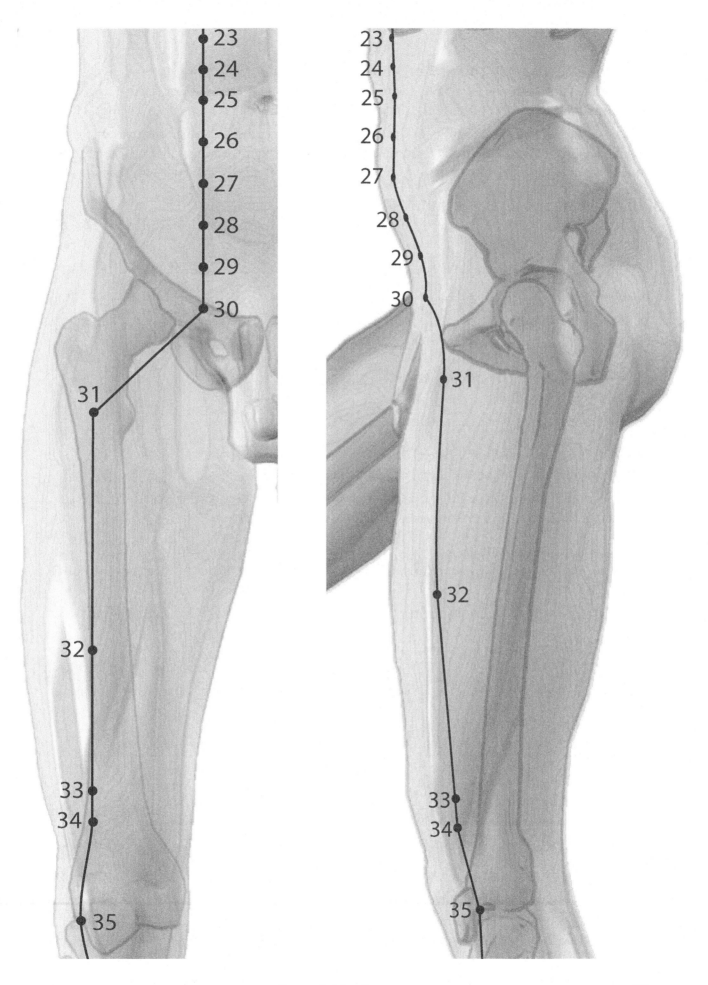

Stomach Meridian

St 36 足三里 Zusanli "Leg Three Miles" - Energy building point.

Start at the lateral edge of the tibia at the angle where the shaft meets the head, then 3 fingers inferior and 3 fingers lateral on the lateral edge of the anterior tibialis.

All Abdominal, Digestive, Nervous Problems, Anorexia, Appendicitis, Arteriosclerosis, Breast Swollen, Constipation, Diabetes, Dizzy, Emaciation, Eye Problems, Fatigue, Flatulence, Headache, Indigestion, Mouth Inflammation, Speaking Difficulty, Tuberculosis, Urinary Suppression.

St 37 上巨虛 Shangjuxu "Upper Great Void"

5 fingers inferior to the angle where the shaft meets the head of the femur, on the lateral edge of the tibia.

Arthritis, Cerebral Anemia, Enterocolitis (Small Intestinal Inflammation), Flatulence, Senility.

St 38 條口 Tiaokou "Ribbon Opening"

5 fingers inferior to St 37.

All Stomach Problems, Arthritis, Bladder Inflammation.

St 39 下巨虛 Xiajuxu "Lower Large Hollow"

3 fingers inferior to St 38.

Blood Disorders, Cerebral Anemia, Senility.

St 40 豐隆 Fenglong "Abundant Bulge"

3 fingers lateral to St 38, on the lateral edge of the anterior tibialis.

Amenorrhea, Asthma, Chest Inflammation, Excessive Mucous, Headache, Liver Abscess, Nasal Discharge Excessive, Nervous Diseases, Pleurisy, Urinary Suppression.

St 41 解谿 Jiexi "Dividing Cleft"

With the foot flexed dorsally/superiorly, the point is located in the niche just lateral to the tibialis attachment.

Abdominal Swelling/Gas, Appendicitis, Constipation, Dizzy, Epilepsy, Headache, Rheumatism.

St 42 沖陽 Chongyang "Surging Yang"

Between the tendons of the 2nd and 3rd toes, 1/2 the distance from St 41 to the base of the toes.

Arthritis, Epilepsy, Gums Inflamed, Swelling with Gas, Tongue Inflamed, Toothache, Vomiting.

St 43 陷谷 Xiangu "Sunken Valley"

Just proximal to the 1st phalange of the 2nd toe, between the 2nd and 3rd metacarpal.

Abdomen Swollen, Eye Congestion, Fever, Flatulence, Hernia, Weakness.

St 44 內庭 Neiting "Inner Court"

On the 1st phalange of the 2nd toe where the shaft meets the proximal head.

Fever, Flatulence, Gums Inflamed, Headache, Hernia, Nasal Problems, Nosebleeds, Weakness.

St 45 厲兌 Lidui "Running Point"

Base of the lateral side of the nail on the 2nd toe.

Abdomen Swollen, Appetite Excessive, Cerebral Anemia, Dementia, Edema, Glands Swollen (Groin), Gums Inflamed, Indigestion, Insomnia, Liver Abscess, Nasal Problems, Nerve Diseases.

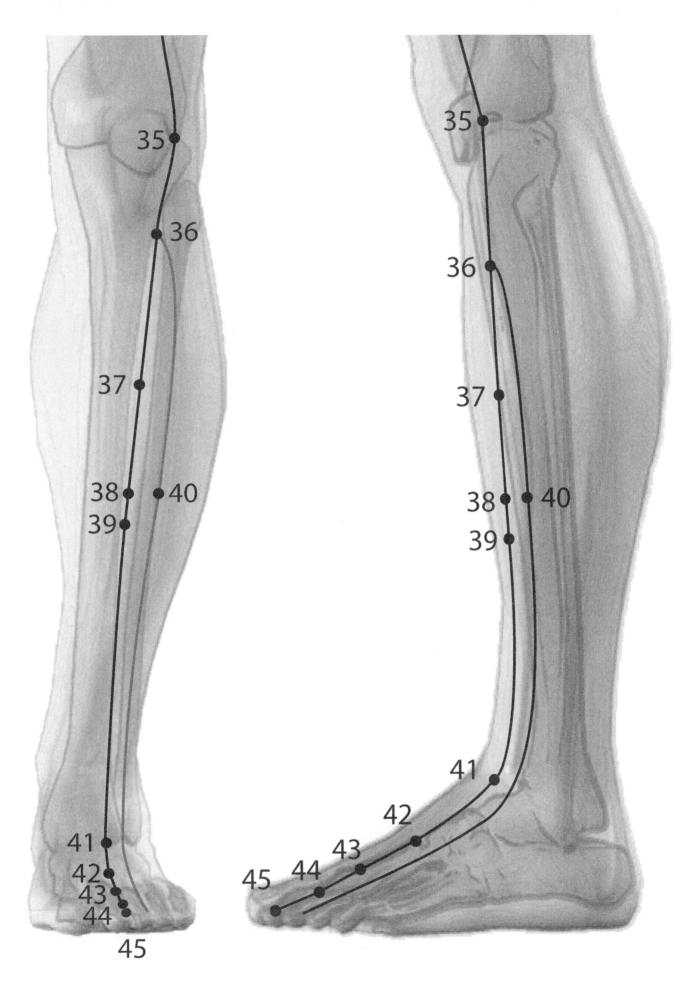

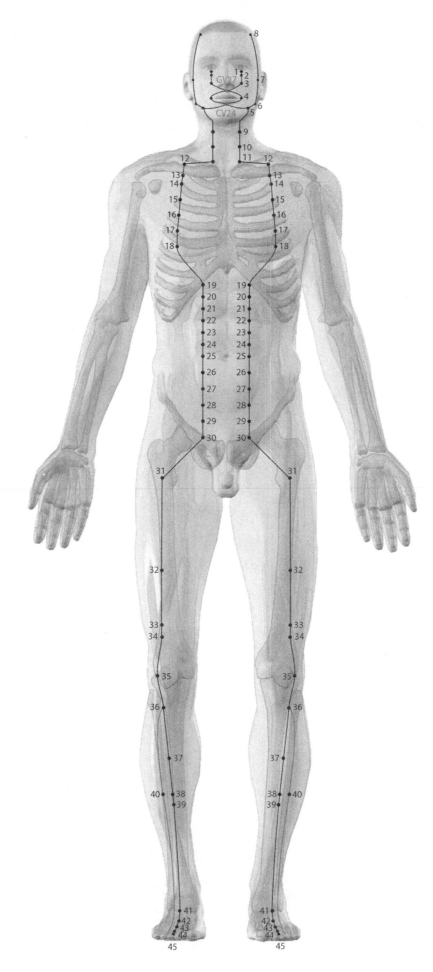

Integrative Acupressure Meridian Atlas

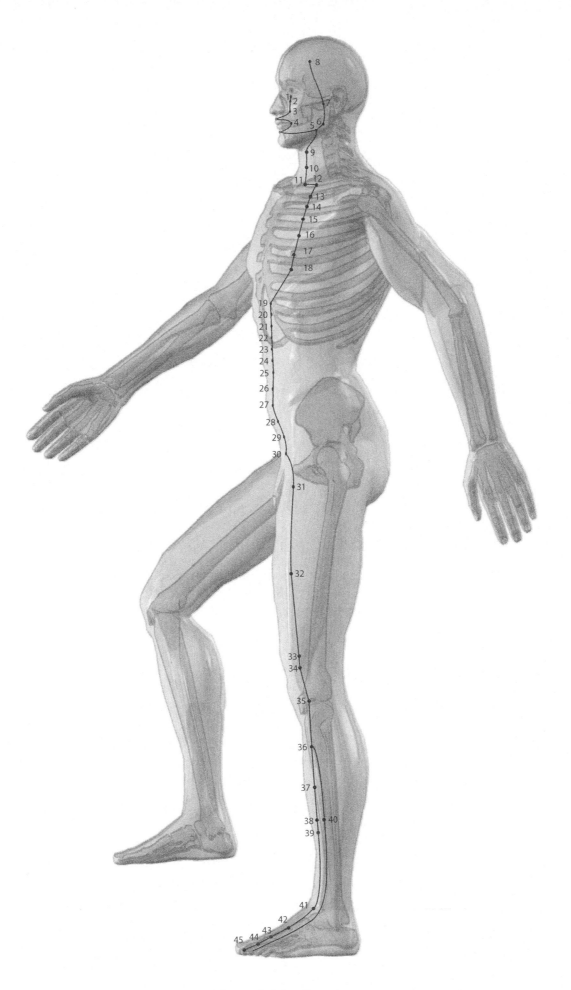

Stomach Meridian

足太陰脾經
Spleen Meridian
of Foot Tai Yin (Greater Yin)

Primary Balancing and Five Element Points

Wood	Sp 1	Well
Fire/Tonification	Sp 2	Spring
Source/Earth/Horary	Sp 3	Stream
Metal/Sedation	Sp 5	River
Water	Sp 9	Sea
Luo	Sp 4	
Accumulation/Xi Cleft	Sp 8	

Key Attributes of the Spleen Meridian

Element: Earth
Season: Late Summer
Stage of Life: Harvest
Climate: Wet
Sense Organ: Taste
Tissue Governed: Muscles, Lymph

Emotions: Worry, Obsession
Balanced Attributes: Bonding, Clarity
Yang Organ: Stomach
Time: 9-11 am
Color: Yellow
Flavor: Sweet

Common Physical Symptoms of Imbalance:

Abdomen (Upper) Distention
Groaning
Yawning
Jaw Tension
Knee Pain, Swelling
Lip, Mouth Sores
Mouth Sideways, Crooked

Neck, Throat Swollen
Vomiting
Abdomen Swollen, Full
Cold in Stomach Area
Frequent Hunger, Thirst
Sleepy After Eating
Abdominal Pain

Common Emotional Symptoms of Imbalance:

Critical
Lack of understanding
Lack of compassion

Anxiety, chronic nervousness tension
The inability to feel emotionally stable, centered

About the Spleen Meridian

The spleen is located within the left part of the abdomen, under the left rib cage. As it does the gallbladder, Western medicine regards the spleen as essentially an expendable organ, though it is known that the immune system is weakened with the loss of the spleen. The spleen performs three functions, according to Western medicine. The first is to create the B- and T-cells of the immune system. Second, the spleen filters the blood and cleanses it of dead cells and bacteria. Third, it acts as a reservoir of blood, releasing extra blood when needed.

From the Western perspective, the spleen is part of the lymphatic system, a vast network of capillaries, ducts, lymph nodes, and trunks. It is similar to the circulatory system but with no central pump like the heart. Instead, the lymph is pumped by movement such as breathing and walking. Because of this, exercise is essential to the proper functioning of the lymphatic system. The lymph system moves fluids and toxins from the cells to the blood, which brings these constituents to the liver for detoxification. The lymph system also absorbs fats from the digestive system and brings them to the blood.

In Traditional Chinese Medicine, the Spleen has a much larger scope. It is said to "separate the pure from the impure," or to determine what should and shouldn't be inside the body through both digestion and the immune system. The Spleen is regarded as the primary organ of digestion and assimilation. Its purview includes the pancreas, which creates digestive enzymes released into the duodenum for breaking down foods to prepare them for digestion. In addition, it manages the blood sugar level through the production of the hormone insulin. It is seen as the governor of digestion and assimilation, and is largely responsible for the proper functioning of the immune system.

Spleen Meridian Point Index

Sp 1 隱白 Yinbai "Hidden White"
Medial proximal corner of the nail of the big toe.

Abdominal Inflammation, Fear & Restlessness (Children), Idiocy, Insomnia, Legs Cold, Pleurisy, Uterine Spasms.

Sp 2 大都 Dadu "Great Pool"
At the base knuckle of the big toe on the medial side, in the niche where the shaft and the knuckle meet.

Fatigue, Fear & Restlessness (Children), Lumbar Pain.

Sp 3 太白 Taibai "Great White"
On the medial side of the big toe, on the underside of the metatarsal where the shaft meets the distal swelling of the bone, also pressing somewhat into muscle underneath. Source Point.

Constipation, Hernia, Indigestion, Intestinal Hemorrhage, Lumbar Pain, Vomiting.

Sp 4 公孫 Gongsun "Grandfather Grandson" (Lo Point)
3 fingers posterior to Sp 3, under the first metatarsal where the shaft meets the proximal head.

Abdominal Swelling, Anorexia, Edema (Head), Epilepsy, Heart Inflammation, Hemorrhoids, Intestinal Hemorrhage, Pleurisy (Chest Inflammation), Stomach Cancer, Vomiting.

Sp 5 商丘 Shangqiu "Metal Mound"

Just anterior to the medial malleolus on the ankle crease, medial to the tendon of the big toe.

Abdominal Distension, Constipation, Cough, Fear & Restlessness (Children), Flatulence, Hemorrhoids, Indigestion, Jaundice, Whooping Cough, Vomiting.

Sp 6 三陰交 Sanyinjiao "Three Yin Intersection"

5 fingers superior to the peak of the malleolus, in the slight niche on the posterior edge of the tibia bone.

All Genital Problems, Anorexia, Edema (head), Hemorrhoids, Indigestion, Insomnia, Nervous Depression, Pain in Leg, Pleurisy (Chest Inflammation), Vomiting.

Sp 7 漏谷 Lougu "Leaking Valley"

4 fingers superior to Sp 6 on the posterior edge of the tibia.

Abdominal Distension, Flatulence, Insomnia, Legs Weak, Psychopathy.

Sp 8 地機 Diji "Earth Cure"

6 fingers proximal to Sp 7, 4 fingers distal to Sp 9 on the posterior edge of the tibia.

Anorexia, Lumbar Pain, Period Painful, Sperm Low, Vaginal Discharge.

Sp 9 陰陵泉 Yinlingquan "Yin Mound Spring"

On the posterior edge of the tibia, in the angle where the shaft meets the head.

Abdomen Cold, Cramp, Insomnia, Legs Weak, Urinary Suppression, Vaginitis.

Sp 10 血海 Xuehai "Sea of Blood"

From the superior medial corner of the patella, 3 fingers superior pressing into the femur.

Abdomen Pain, Period Painful, Pleurisy, Testicle Inflammation, Womb Inflammation.

Sp 11 箕門 Jimen "Separation Gate"

7 fingers superior to Sp 10.

Bladder Problems, Mucous Discharge, Swollen Glands (Groin).

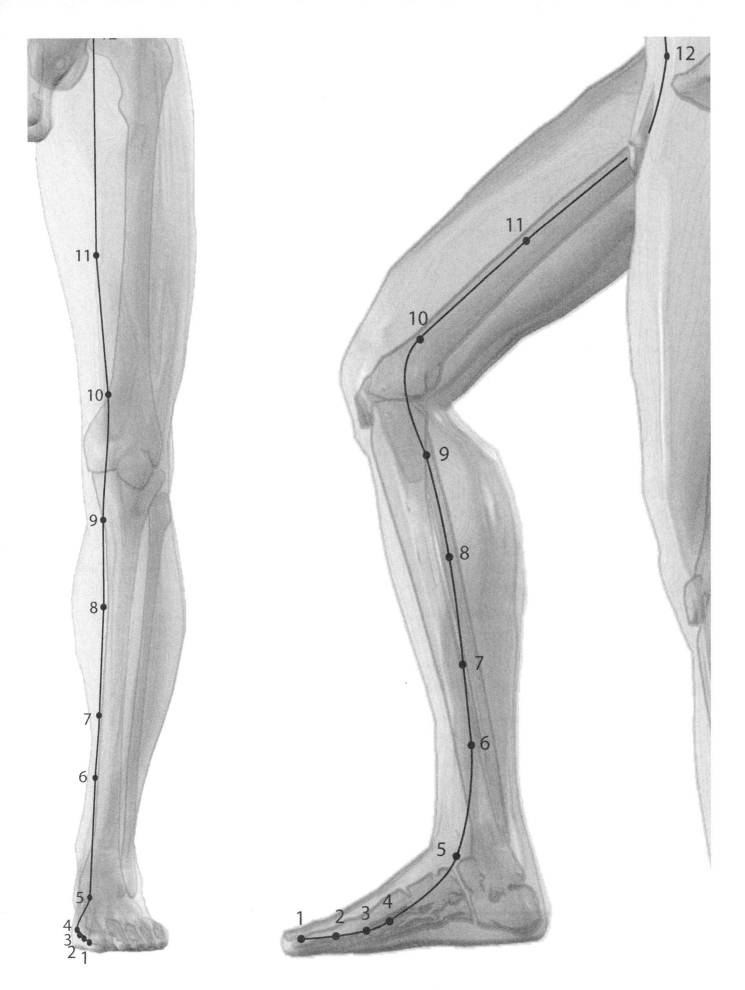

Spleen Meridian

Sp 12 沖門 Chongmen "Surging Gate"

4 fingers lateral to the corner of the pubic bone, just inferior to the inguinal ligament.

Abdominal Distension, Mucous Discharge; Breast, Testicle or Womb Inflammation.

Sp 13 府舍 Fushe "Bowel Abode"

Just superior to the inguinal ligament, 3 fingers superior to Sp 12.

Cecum Inflammation, Cholera, Constipation, Spleen Inflammation.

Sp 14 腹結 Fujie "Abdomen Stagnation"

5 fingers inferior to Sp 12.

Abdominal Inflammation, Colic, Cough, Diarrhea, Genital Problems, Legs Weak.

Sp 15 大橫 Da heng "Great Horizontal"

6 fingers lateral to the umbilicus.

Constipation, Diarrhea (Chronic), Enterocolitis (Acute), Influenza, Sweat Excessive.

Sp 16 腹哀 Fuai "Abdomen Suffering"

5 fingers lateral to the midline where you touch the edge of the rib cage, in the niche between the attachment of the 9th and 10th ribs.

Blood in Stools, Intestinal Hemorrhage, Stomach Hyperacid, Ulcer.

Sp 17 食竇 Shidou "Food Cavity"

3 fingers/1 intercostal space inferior to Sp 18.

Liver Pain (Ribs on Right Side), Pleurisy, Pneumonia.

Sp 18 天谿 Tianxi "Celestial Cleft"

Between the 4th and 5th ribs where the front and side of the chest meet. 5 fingers inferior to the front of the armpit between the 4th and 5th ribs just outside the breast.

Breast Inflammation, Bronchitis, Lactation Insufficient, Pneumonia.

Sp 19 胸鄉 Xiongxiang "Chest Village"

1 rib (3 fingers) superior to Sp 18 between the 3rd and 4th ribs.

Anorexia, Bronchitis, Chest Congestion, Esophagus Contraction.

Sp 20 周榮 Zhourong "Complete Nourishment"

3 fingers superior to Sp 19 between the 2nd and 3rd ribs, 2 fingers inferior to Lu 1.

Anorexia, Bronchitis, Chest Congestion, Esophagus Contraction.

Sp 21 大包 Dabao "Great Embrace"

In the intercostal space between the 6th and 7th ribs where the front and side of the rib cage meet. 4 fingers posterior and 3 fingers inferior to Sp 17.

Digestive Problems, Endocarditis (Inflammation of Tissue Surrounding Heart).

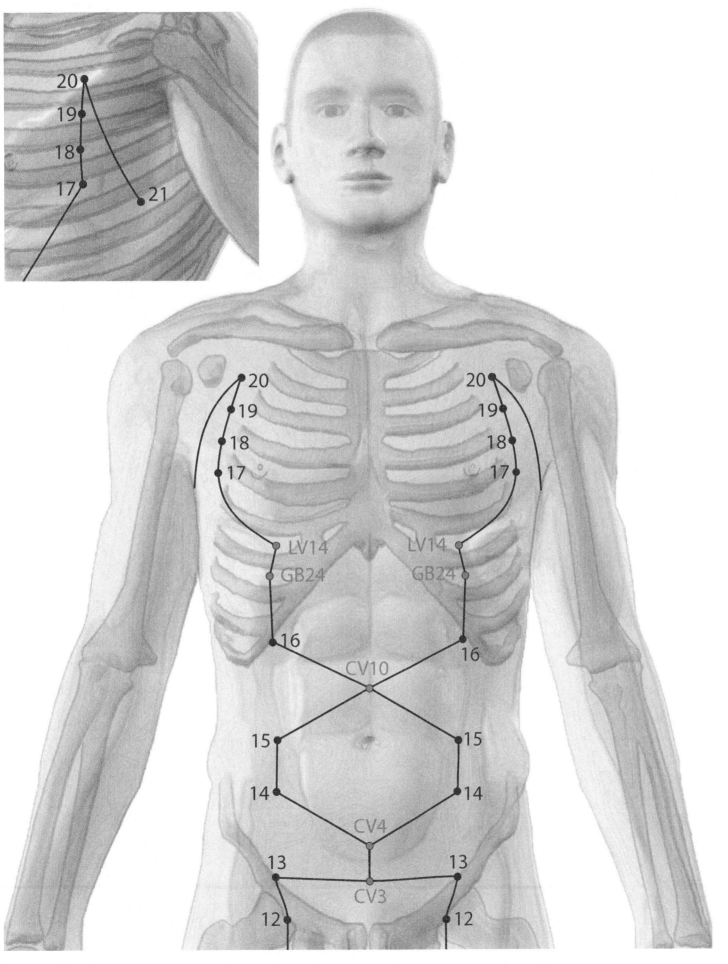

Spleen Meridian

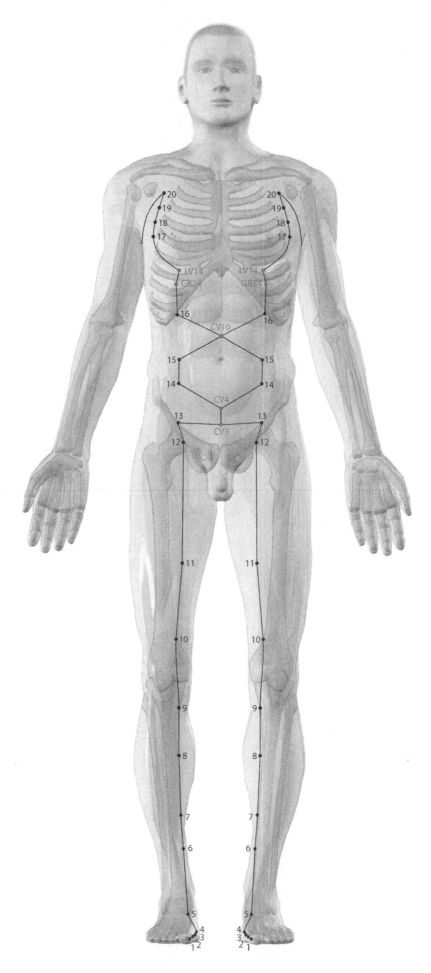

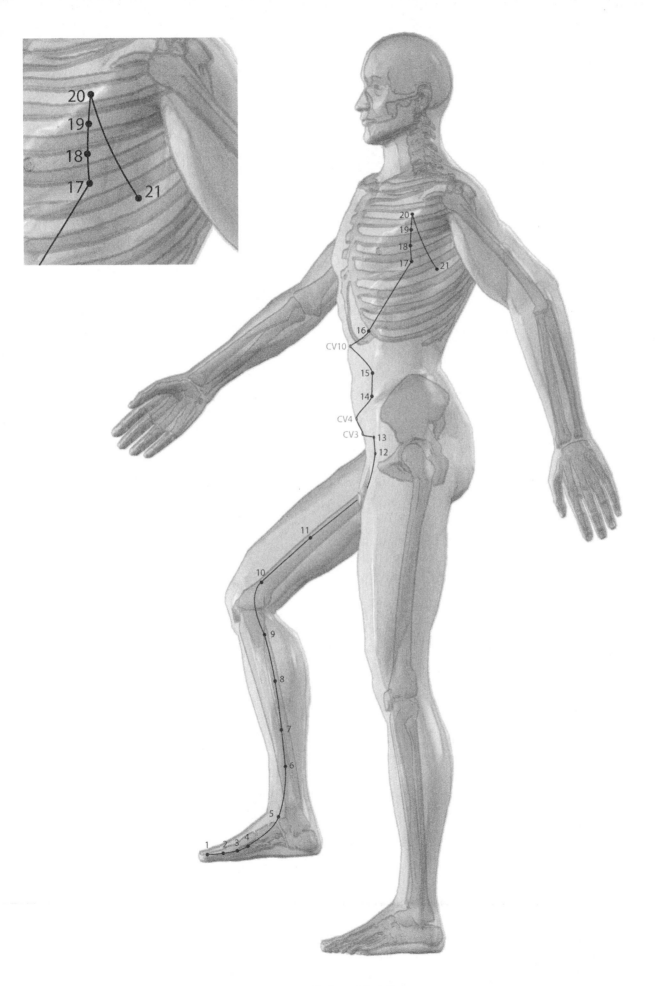

手少陰心經
Heart Meridian
of Hand Shao Yin (Lesser Yin)

Primary Balancing and Five Element Points

Wood/Tonification	Ht 9	Well
Fire/Horary	Ht 8	Spring
Source/Earth/Sedation	Ht 7	Stream
Metal	Ht 4	River
Water	Ht 3	Sea
Luo	Ht 5	
Accumulation/Xi Cleft	Ht 6	

Key Attributes of the Heart Meridian

Element: Fire
Season: Summer
Stage of Life: Growth
Climate: Hot
Sense Organ: Tongue
Tissue Governed: Blood

Emotion: Joy
Balanced Attribute: Contentment
Yang Organ: Small Intestine
Time: 11am - 1pm
Color: Red
Flavor: Spicy, Bitter

Common Physical Symptoms of Imbalance:

Hot or cold hands and feet
Nervousness, Irritability
Red Complexion
Mental Or Emotional Disturbance
Insomnia
Disturbed Sleep

Excessive Dreaming
Cardiovascular Disorders
Brain Or Nervous System Disorders
Speech Problems
Spontaneous Sweating
Poor Memory of Important Life Events

Common Emotional Symptoms of Imbalance:

Excessive Laughter (Excess)
Hysteria (Excess)

Expressionless Appearance (Deficiency)
Lack of Joy (Deficiency)

About the Heart Meridian

In Western physiology the heart is the pump that moves blood through our circulatory system. The heart, located behind the sternum, is actually two pumps, each one perfectly coordinated with the other. The left side of the heart serves as a pump for the general circulation, pumping oxygen-rich blood to every cell in the body. The right side pumps venous blood, carrying carbon dioxide, to the lungs.

Because the job of pumping blood to the general circulation is much more difficult—there's a lot more resistance and a lot more distance to travel—the left side of the heart is more muscular, stronger, and larger. On average, the heart beats 60 to 80 times per minute, cycling the entire blood supply of the body through the heart in 60 seconds.

In the West, we also associate the heart on an emotional level with love and caring, with compassion and an openness to the feelings and well-being of others. This is actually very similar to the Traditional Chinese Medicine understanding of the Heart.

In the Eastern view, the Heart corresponds to the heart as a pump for the blood, but it is also very much tied to the overall "tenor" and functioning of the nervous system, or what we call the balance of the mind. The Heart is called "the palace of the Shen," or the home of the spirit. It influences your "spirit," but not the ghostly kind – more accurately your state of mind. If the Shen is strong, that corresponds with clear thinking, wisdom and connection. If the Shen is weak, there is confusion and disturbed thoughts and feelings.

You can see the quality of the Shen in the eyes. Strong Shen shows as bright, alive eyes whereas when the Shen is weak the eyes appear dull and lifeless.

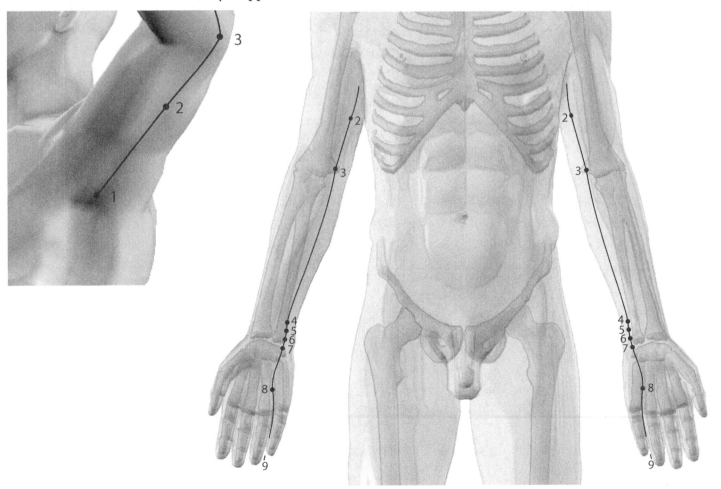

Heart Meridian Point Index

Ht 1 極泉 Jiquan "Highest Spring"

Located in the center of the deepest part of the armpit with the arm down. Press laterally into the head of the humerus bone.

Depression, Dry Heaves, Heart Inflammation, Hysteria.

Ht 2 青靈 Qingling "Green Spirit"

Midway between the elbow (Ht 3) and the armpit (Ht 1). Proximally 7 fingers from Ht 3 on the humerus bone.

Coldness, Fever, Headache, Intercostal Pain, Sadness, Depression. The French call this the "Joi de Vivre" (Joy of Life) point.

Ht 3 少海 Shaohai "Lesser Sea"

Located at the inside crease of the elbow just anterior to the head of the ulna. If you mark 3 evenly spaced points from inside to outside, Ht 3 is the medial (pinky) side point, Pc 3 is in the middle, and Lu 5 is on the lateral (thumb) side.

Dizziness, Fingers Cold, Facial or Intercostal Neuralgia, Glandular Disorders, Swollen Glands, Headache, Parkinson's Disease, Pleurisy, Psychopathy, Pulmonary Tuberculosis, Toothache.

Ht 4-7 are each 2 tight fingers apart, and located just to the lateral (thumb) side of the tendon m. flexor carpi ulnaris that runs over the head of the ulna bone. To find 4, 5 and 6 start from Ht 7.

Ht 4 靈道 Lingdao "Spirit Path"

A tight 2 fingers proximal to Ht 5 along the same line.

Dry Heaves, Elbow Arthritis, Endocardium Inflamed, Hysteria, Sudden Muteness.

Ht 5 通里 Tongli "Inward Connection"

A tight 2 fingers proximal to Ht 6, where the ulnar shaft meets the head.

Anxiety, Dizziness, Headache, Menstrual Cramps, Psychopathy, Sore Throat, Sudden Muteness, Tonsillitis, Urinary Incontinence, Uterine Hemorrhage.

Ht 6 陰郄 Yinxi "Yin Cleft"

A tight 2 fingers proximal to Ht 7 on the point of the ulnar head, just lateral to the tendon.

Anxiety, Dizziness, Fever With Chills, Headache, Nosebleed, Vaginal Discharge, Vomiting Blood, Womb Inflammation.

Ht 7 神門 Shenmen "Spirit Gate", Heart Source point

In the medial (pinky side) crease of the wrist just lateral to the attachment of the tendon. Slightly push the tendon medially to reach Ht 7 underneath.

Anorexia, Anxiety, Epilepsy, Heart Swollen, Insomnia, Phlegm Excessive, Postpartum Hemorrhage, Psychopathy, Scrofula, Tongue Paralysis, Tonsillitis.

Ht 8 少府 Shaofu "Lesser Mansion"

Located between the 4th & 5th metatarsals where the tip of the pinky touches the hand when making a fist.

Anxiety, Arm Pain, Period Excessive, Urinary Incontinence, Vaginal Itch.

Ht 9 少沖 Shaochong "Lesser Surge"

On the lateral (thumb) side of the pinky, the lateral corner of the base of the nail.

Heart Attack Revival, Anxiety, Depression, Intercostal Pain, Melancholy, Pleurisy, Restlessness, Stroke, Swollen & Sore Throat, Weakness after Fever.

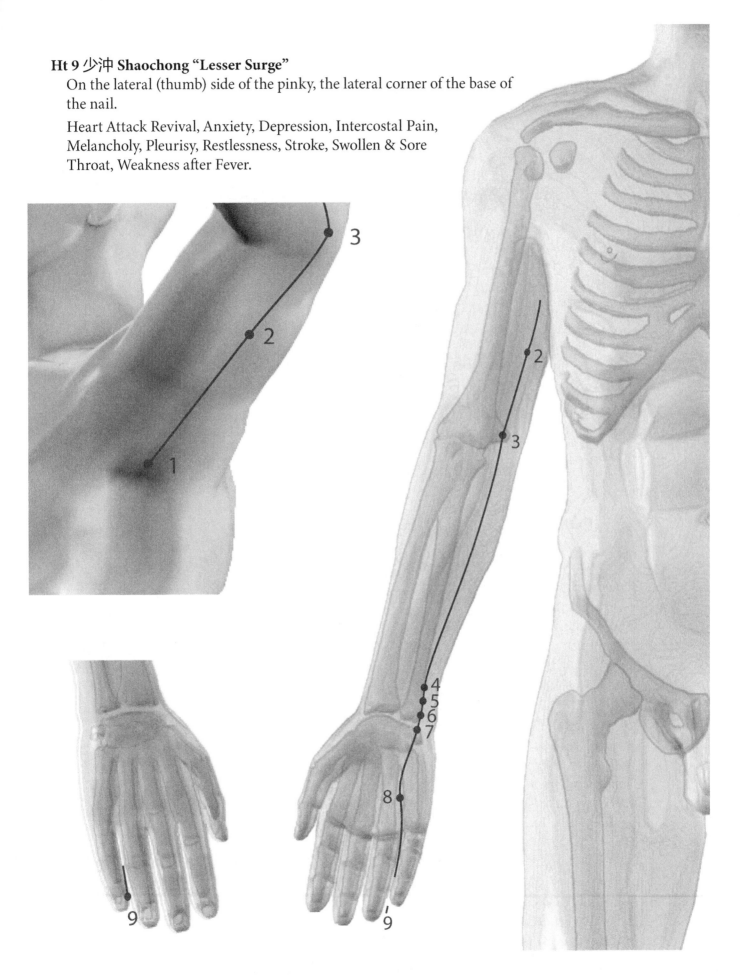

手太陽小腸經
Small Intestine Meridian
of Hand Tai Yang (Greater Yang)

Primary Balancing and Five Element Points

Metal	SI 1	Well
Water	SI 2	Spring
Wood/Tonification	SI 3	Stream
Fire/Horary	SI 5	River
Earth/Sedation	SI 8	Sea
Source	SI 4	
Luo	SI 7	
Accumulation/Xi Cleft	SI 6	

Key Attributes of the Small Intestine Meridian

Element: Fire

Season: Summer

Stage of Life: Growth

Climate: Hot

Sense Organ: Tongue

Tissue Governed: Blood

Emotion: Joy

Balanced Attribute: Contentment

Yin Organ: Heart

Time: 1-3 pm

Color: Red

Flavor: Spicy, Bitter

Common Physical Symptoms of Imbalance:

Abdomen (Lower) Distended

Arm Pain As If Broken

Cheeks Swollen

Head Difficult to Turn To Side

Shoulder Pain, Tension

Swellings or Nodules between Tendons

Elbow Joint Stiff Or Sore

Eyes Sore, Red

Disorders related to the small intestine, including Crohn's Disease

Common Emotional Symptoms of Imbalance:

Lack of mental clarity or judgment (Deficiency)

Lack of joy (Deficiency)

Excessively Emotional (Excess)

Hysteria (Excess)

About the Small Intestine Meridian

The small intestine is approximately 7 meters long, a tortuous tube winding through your lower abdomen. The two purposes of the small intestine are, first, to break down food to prepare it for absorption and second, to absorb nutrients from the food into the bloodstream (mostly) and the lymphatic system (fats). The small intestine consists of three parts:

The duodenum, about 30 centimeters long, starts at the pyloric sphincter of the stomach. Food that has been broken down by chewing, saliva, and the stomach acids proceeds to the duodenum where bile from the liver breaks down fats and oils, along with enzymes produced by the pancreas including trypsin and chymotrypsin to digest proteins; amylase for the digestion of carbohydrates; and lipase to break down fats. The duodenum also absorbs some nutrients.

The jejunum, approximately 2.5 meters long, absorbs vitamins, minerals, carbohydrates and proteins (into the vascular system) and fats (into the lymph capillaries).

The ileum, about 4 meters long, absorbs any final nutrients, with major absorptive products being vitamin B12 and bile acids which are then recycled to the liver. The ileum ends at the ileocecal valve which allows digested food (chyme) to move into the large intestine but does not allow backflow into the small intestine.

The small intestine's work of digesting and absorbing nutrients is assisted by the presence of trillions of bacteria, many of which aid in the breakdown of food particles. Food takes an average of five to six hours to pass through the small intestine.

In Chinese medicine, it's said that the Small Intestine is "the official in charge of receiving, filling, and transforming," not unlike the Western view. It is seen as linked with the heart, helping it to bring clarity of mind, distinguishing and assimilating good ideas.

Small Intestine Meridian Point Index

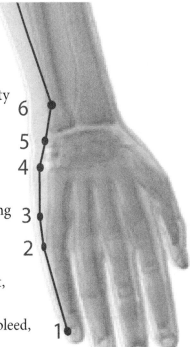

SI 1 少澤 Shaoze "Lesser Marsh"
On the medial (pinky) side of the pinky distal phalanx bone, medial corner of the base of the nail.

Heart Attack Revival, Breast Inflammation, Cough, Headache, Heart Dilated, Insomnia, Lactation Insufficient, Stroke, Tonsillitis, Vision Misty

SI 2 前谷 Qiangu "Front Valley"
Just distal to the head of the fifth proximal phalange where the side and top of the finger meet.

Breast Inflammation, Cough (Obstinate), Ears Ring, Epilepsy, Itching, Lactation Insufficient, Nose Stuffy, Tonsillitis, Vision Obscured, Vomiting Blood.

SI 3 後谿 Houxi "Back Stream"
Just proximal to the head of the fifth proximal phalange, where the shaft, proximal head and abductor digiti mini manus muscle meet.

Cornea Inflammation, Deafness, Epilepsy, Itching, Neck Twisted, Nosebleed, Tonsillitis.

SI 4 腕骨 Wangu "Wrist Bone"

On the medial (pinky) side of the hand in the niche between 5th metacarpal and the triquetrum bones, at the edge of the abductor digiti mini manus muscle.

Arm Arthritis, Cornea Inflammation, Ears Ring, Headache, Jaw Inflammation, Tears Excessive or Deficient, Vomiting.

SI 5 陽谷 Yanggu "Yang Valley"

In the medial crease of the wrist between the head of the ulna and the carpus bone pressing toward the pisiform bone.

Canker & Gum Sores, Deafness, Ears Ring, Epilepsy, Fear & Anxiety (Children), Glands Swollen (Groin).

SI 6 養老 Yanglao "Support the Aged"

On the medial side of the ulna, 3 fingers proximal to SI 5 where the shaft of the ulna meets the head.

Arm Paralysis, Eye Congestion, Vision Weakening.

SI 7 支正 Zhizheng "Branch of Upright"

7 fingers proximal to SI 6, on the edge of the ulna.

Cyst on Eyelid, Facial Congestion, Headache, Psychopathy, Thinking Poor.

SI 8 小海 Xiaohai "Small Sea"

Between the olecranon process (the point on the elbow when the arm is bent) and the medial condyle of the humerus, where the ulnar nerve is exposed (the "funny bone").

Arm Spasm, Deafness, Glands Swollen, Gums Inflamed.

SI 9 肩貞 Jianzhen "True Shoulder"

Just under the teres major muscle pressing into the lateral side of the scapula, follow along the side of the scapula starting level with the bottom of the armpit to where the scapula curves laterally; SI 9 is in the angle of the curve, pressing medially and somewhat superiorly.

Arm & Shoulder Pain & Tension, Deafness, Ears Ring, Headache.

SI 10 臑俞 Naoshu "Upper arm transporter"

5 fingers superior to SI 9, just inferior to the spine of the scapula and medial to the sharp point at the lateral head of the scapula spine.

Scapula Pain, Shoulder, Pain.

SI 11 天宗 Tianzong "Heavenly Gathering"

In the center of the scapula, 2 fingers down from the spine of the scapula.

Neck Pain & Spasm.

SI 12 秉風 Bingfeng "Grasping the Wind"

4 fingers directly superior to SI 11 and just superior to the spine of the scapula.

Scapula Pain & Spasm.

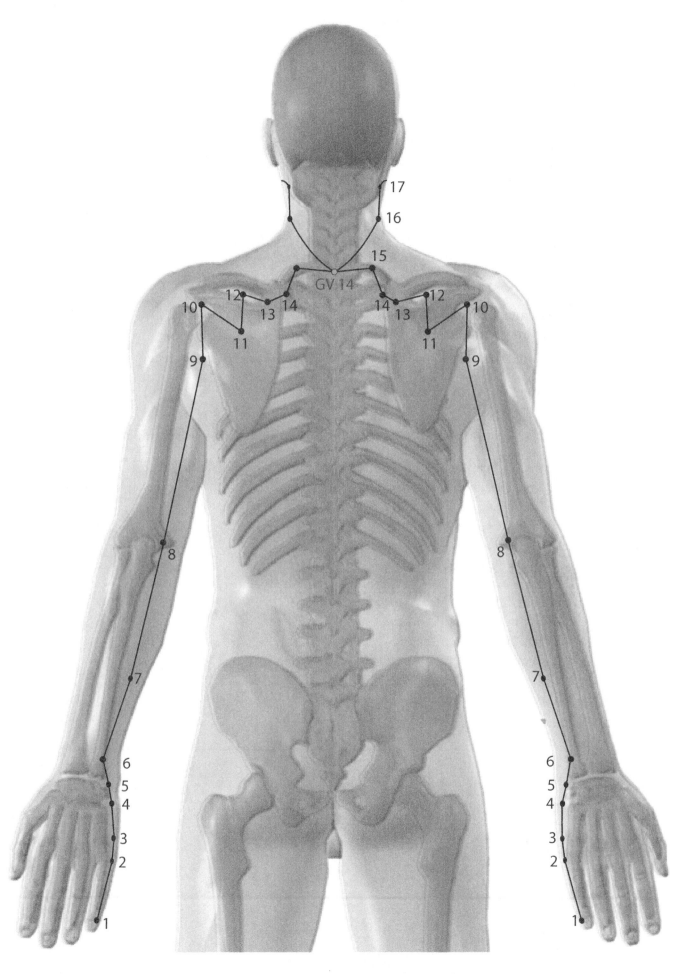

Small Intestine Meridian

SI 13 曲垣 Quyuan "Crooked Wall"
3 fingers medial and 1.5 fingers inferior to SI 12. Directly inferior to the medial superior angle (sharp point) of the scapula.

Arm Paralysis, Forearm & Elbow Pain.

SI 14 肩外俞 Jianwaishu "Outer Shoulder Transporter"
On the medial edge of the scapula, 2 fingers medially and 2 fingers superior to SI 13

Arm Paralysis, Pleurisy, Pneumonia.

SI 15 肩中俞 Jianzhongshu "Middle Shoulder Transporter"
3 fingers superior and 2 fingers medial to SI 14; 2 finger superior and 2 fingers lateral to Bl 11.

Breathing Difficulty, Bronchitis, Dizziness, Vision Weakening.

SI 16 天窗 Tianchuang "Heavenly Window"
5 fingers inferior and 2 fingers posterior to SI 17.

Deafness, Ears Ring, Gums Inflamed, Jaw Inflamed, Neck Pain, Neck Twisted.

SI 17 天容 Tianrong "Heavenly Appearance"
Just posterior to the posterior angle of the lower jaw, pressing medially.

Cyst under Tongue, Deafness, Dizziness, Ears Ring, Gums Inflamed, Neck Pain, Pleurisy.

SI 18 顴髎 Quanliao "Cheek Bone Crevice"
Follow the zygoma (cheekbone) from the nose down and over to the most inferior point of the zygoma, then just behind in the curve formed by zygoma and zygomatic arch.

Facial Spasm, Upper Teeth Pain.

SI 19 聽宮 Tinggong "Palace of Hearing"
2 fingers anterior and 2 fingers inferior to the tragus (ear flap that protects the ear canal) (TW 21 is just in front of the tragus and 2 fingers above, GB 2 is 2 fingers below 19 just in front of the bottom of ear).

Deafness, Ears Ring, Throat Sore.

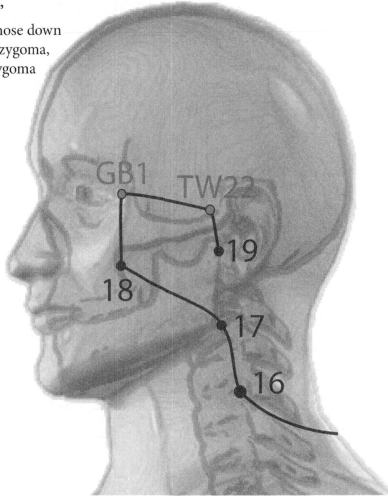

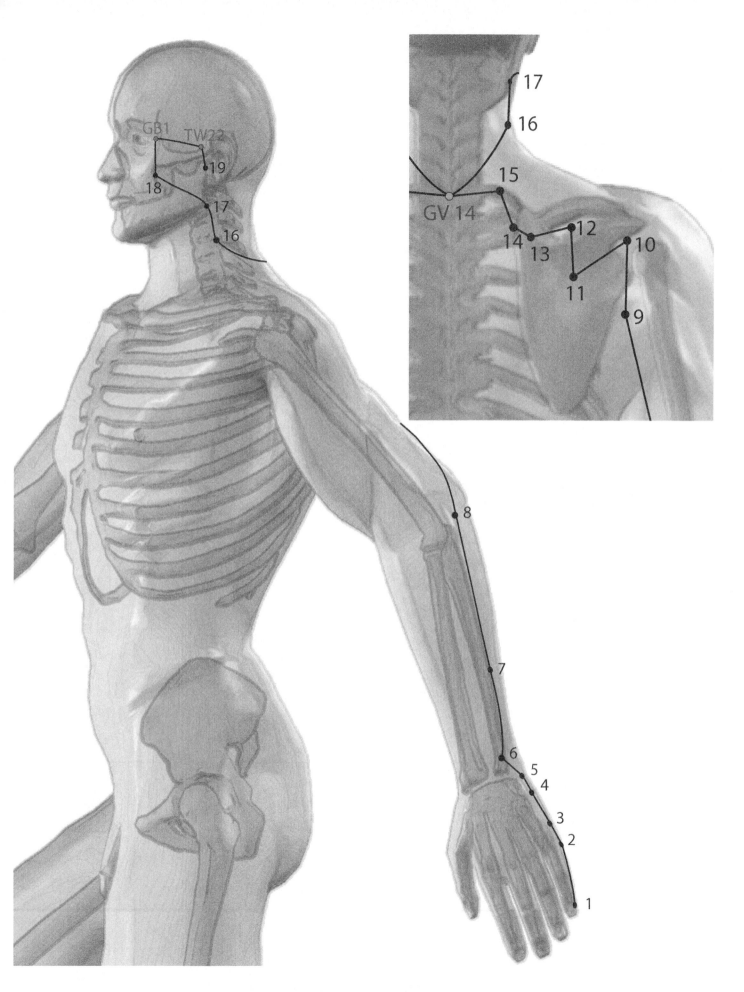

足太陽膀胱經
Bladder Meridian
of Foot Tai Yang (Greater Yang)

Primary Balancing and Five Element Points

Metal/Tonification	Bl 67	Well
Water/Horary	Bl 66	Spring
Wood/Sedation	Bl 65	Stream
Fire	Bl 60	River
Earth	Bl 40	Sea
Source	Bl 64	
Luo	Bl 58	
Accumulation/Xi Cleft	Bl 64	

Key Attributes of the Bladder Meridian

Element: Water
Season: Winter
Stage of Life: Storage
Climate: Cold
Sense Organ: Hearing
Tissue Governed: Bones, Hair on Head

Emotions: Fear, Anxiety
Balanced Attributes: Courage
Yin Organ: Kidney
Time: 3-4 pm
Color: Black/Blue
Flavor: Salty

Common Physical Symptoms of Imbalance:

Back Problems
Bladder Infection
Fevers, Intermittent Headaches
Incontinence
Hip or Sacrum Problems
Mania

Eye Pain on Inside Corner
Paranoia
Shoulders Rounded
Back of Calf Pain, Spasm
Feet Hurt After Standing
Toe Stiff (Little)

Common Emotional Symptoms of Imbalance:

Chronic Anxiety
Excessive Suspicion
Fear

Foolhardiness
Jealousy
Long-standing Grudges

About the Bladder Meridian

From the Western perspective, the bladder is a round sac composed of three layers of muscle. It is located in the lower abdomen, behind the pubic bone. The bladder stores and secretes urine—it holds about a pint of liquid waste—that originates from the kidneys. As the bladder fills with urine and expands, it sends signals through the spinal cord to the brain, which in turn creates the impulse to urinate.

In Chinese Medicine, in addition to its function of storing the urine, the Bladder Meridian controls how fluids are transformed during urine production. The Bladder's capabilities and functions are intertwined and dependent on the Kidney energy, specifically the Kidney Yang. If the Kidney is Yang Deficient, the Bladder may not have the sufficient Qi and Heat to transform fluids properly into urine. This could result in overly clear urine that must be excreted more frequently.

Another important function of the Bladder Meridian is as a host to the Shu points on the back, which correspond to all 12 of the Organs as well as certain structures, and are often tender, swollen or knotted when there is an issue with that particular Organ.

The Bladder Meridian, along with the Gall Bladder Meridian, are the longest meridians of the body, extending from the head to the feet.

Bladder Meridian Point Index

Bl 1 睛明 Jingming "Bright Eyes"
The medial orbit of the eye just above the canthus (small bump on the inside of the eye).

All Eye Problems

Bl 2 攢竹 Zanzhu "Gathered Bamboo"
inside of the eyebrow on the edge of the eye orbit in a little niche, 2 fingers lateral to the midline.

Eyes Excess Tears or Vision Obscured, Headache, Head Pain (Front).

Bl 3 眉衝 Meichong "Eyebrows' Ascension"
Straight up to the hairline from Bl 2.

Blind Spot In Vision, Epilepsy, Headache.

Bl 4 曲差 Quchai "Deviating Curve"
2 fingers lateral to Bl 3. GB 15 is 2 tight fingers lateral to Bl 4, directly above the pupil of the eye.

Facial Pain, Headache, Nosebleed.

Bl 5 五處 Wuchu "Fifth Position"
3 fingers posterior to Bl 4.

Headache, Dizziness, Hemiplegia, Epilepsy

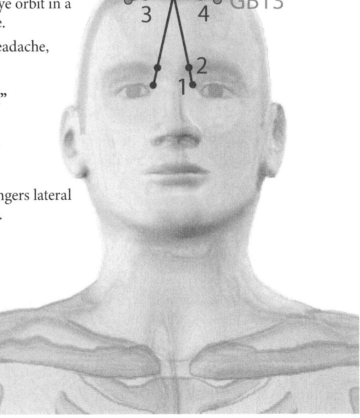

The meridian runs back along the head to the neck from here, 2 fingers laterally from the midline

Bl 6 承光 Chengguang "Receiving Light"

3 fingers posterior to Bl 5.

Chills, Headache.

Bl 7 通天 Tongtian "Reaching Upward"

3 fingers posterior to Bl 6.

Bronchitis, Nosebleed, Shock.

Bl 8 絡卻 Luoque "Declining Connection"

3 fingers posterior to Bl 7, the farthest back on the top of the head before starting to descend.

Ears Ring, Nervous Exhaustion, Psychopathy.

Bl 9 玉枕 Yuzhen "Jade Pillow"

7 fingers inferiorly from Bl 8, 5 fingers superior to Bl 10, 3 tight fingers from the midline.

Cerebral Congestion, Headache, Myopia, Sweat Excessive.

Bl 10 天柱 Tianzhu "Upper Pillar"

At the base of the occiput 3 tight fingers lateral to the midline, just inside of the trapezius attachment.

Depression, Nosebleed, Vaginal Infection.

Bl 11 大杼 Dazhu "Great Vertebra"

3 fingers lateral to the space between the 1st and 2nd thoracic vertebrae spinous processes, at the tip of the 1st thoracic transverse process.

Bone Disease, Bronchitis, Epilepsy, Joint Pain, Knee Arthritis.

The rest of the meridian follows down the spine just outside the tips of the transverse processes, between the spinous processes of the vertebrae listed—note that the spinous process of a vertebra is lower than its transverse process. Each point on the inner Bladder channel is two fingers out from the spinous process, just inside the vertical band of the erector spinae.

Bl 12 風門 Fengmen "Wind Gate" Reunion of all Yang Meridians.

At the transverse process of the 2nd thoracic, between the spinous processes of T2-3.

Asthma, Bronchitis, Cancer, Post-Chill or Freezing, Nasal Problems, Sleep Excessive, Whooping Cough.

Bl 13 肺俞 Feishu "Lung Transporter"

At the transverse process of the 3rd thoracic, between the spinous processes of T3-4. Lung Shu point.

Bronchitis, Insomnia, Jaundice, Pericarditis (Inflammation of the Pericardium), Pneumonia, Pulmonary Tuberculosis, Skin Eruptions or Problems.

Bl 14 厥陰俞 Jueyinshu "Absolute yin Transporter"

At the transverse process of the 4th thoracic. Pericardium Shu point.

Cough (Chronic), Pericarditis, Toothache, Vascular Problems.

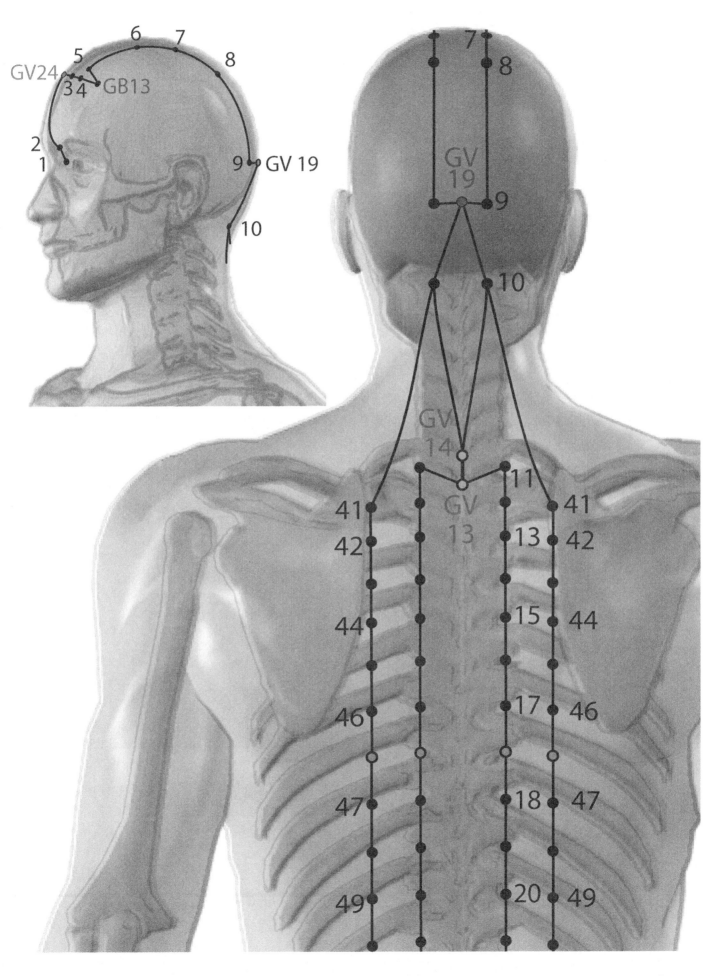

Bl 15 心俞 Xinshu "Heart Transporter"

At the transverse process of the 5th thoracic. This is the Heart Shu point.

Epilepsy, Heart Problems, Speech Difficulties, Throat Constricted.

Bl 16 督俞 Dushu "Governor Transporter"

At the transverse process of the 6th thoracic. This is the Governing Vessel Shu point.

Colic, Nervous Problems, Pericarditis.

Bl 17 膈俞 Geshu "Diaphragm Transporter"

At the transverse process of the 7th thoracic. This is the Diaphragm Shu point.

Any Stricture or Constriction, Anorexia, Breathing & Lung Problems, Depression, Edema, Fatigue in Limbs, Heart Problems, Internal Bleeding, Intestinal Problems, Night Sweats, Skin Problems, Stomach & Digestive Problems.

Between 17 & 18 is an extra point called the glucose point in Integrative Acupressure. It gets tight when there's any problem with blood sugar or sugar sensitivity, hence I call it the Pancreas Shu.

Bl 18 肝俞 Ganshu "Liver Transporter"

At the transverse process of the 9th thoracic. This is the Liver Shu point.

Bronchitis, Eye Problems, Fat Digestion Problems, Jaundice, Liver Problems, Psychopathy, Toxicity, Ulcer (Duodenal).

Bl 19 膽俞 Danshu "Gallbladder Transporter"

At the transverse process of the 10th thoracic. Gall Bladder Shu point.

Chills, Colic, Gallbladder Problems, Glands Swollen, Hypertension, Jaundice, Pharyngitis, Skin Dry.

Bl 20 脾俞 Pishu "Spleen Transporter"

At the transverse process of the 11th thoracic. Spleen Shu point.

Breathing Difficulty, Diabetes, Diarrhea, Jaundice, Edema, Lymph Problems.

Bl 21 胃俞 Weishu "Stomach Transporter"

At the transverse process of the 12th thoracic. Stomach Shu point.

Abdominal Distension, Colitis, Digestive Problems, Liver Problems, Stomach Cancer.

Bl 22 三焦俞 Sanjiaoshu "Sanjiao Transporter"

At the transverse process of the 1st lumbar vertebra. Triple Warmer Shu point, associated with the adrenals.

Adrenal Exhaustion, Anorexia, Depression, Digestive Problems, Endocrine Glands, Intestinal Inflammation, Kidney Inflammation, Sexual Problems.

Bl 23 腎俞 Shenshu "Kidney Transporter"

At the transverse process of the 2nd lumbar. Kidney Shu point.

Diabetes, Emaciation, Headache, Hemorrhoids, Kidney & Urinary Problems, Liver Problems, Nervous Problems, Periods Painful, Sexual Problems, Teeth Grinding, Weakness.

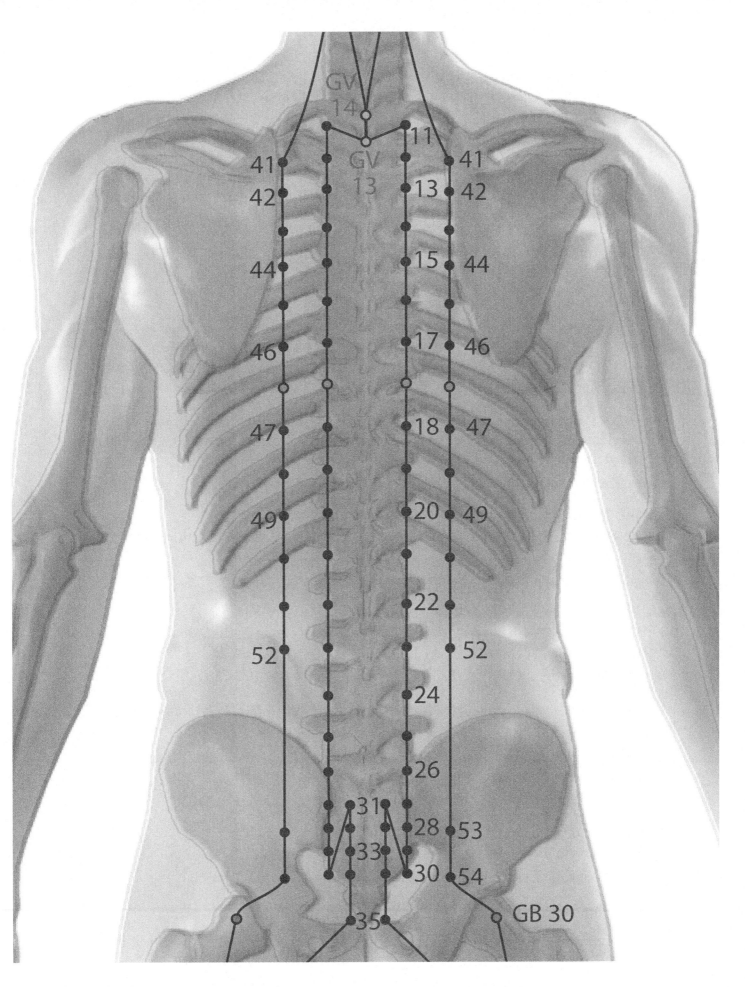

Bl 24 氣海俞 Qihaishu "Sea of Qi Transporter"
At the transverse process of the 3rd lumbar. Upper Lumbar Shu point.

Hemorrhoids, Hypertension, Low Back Pain.

Bl 25 大腸俞 Dachangshu "Large Intestine Transporter"
At the transverse process of the 4th lumbar. Large Intestine Shu point.

Abdominal Distension, Cecum Inflamed, Constipation (Chronic), Diarrhea, Intestinal Inflammation, Kidney Inflammation, Urinary Incontinence.

Bl 26 關元俞 Guanyuanshu "Gate of Origin Transporter"
At the transverse process of the 5th lumbar. Lower Lumbar Shu point.

Anuria, Diarrhea, Leg & Low Back Pain.

Bl 27 小腸俞 Xiaochangshu "Small Intestine Transporter"
3 fingers lateral to the 1st sacral spinous process and slightly inferior, on the first sacral foramen. Small Intestine Shu point.

Constipation, Diarrhea, Hemorrhoids, Hernia, Intestinal Inflammation, Mucous Discharge.

Bl 28 膀胱俞 Pangguangshu "Bladder Transporter"
3 fingers lateral to the 2nd sacral spinous process and slightly inferior, on the second sacral foramen. Bladder Shu point.

Bladder Infection, Constipation, Diabetes, Diarrhea, Urinary Incontinence.

Bl 29 中膂俞 Zhonglushu "Mid-Spine Transporter"
3 fingers lateral to the 3rd sacral spinous process and slightly inferior, on the third sacral foramen. Sacrum Shu point.

Diabetes, Intestinal Inflammation, Sacrum & Leg Problems.

Bl 30 白環俞 Baihuanshu "White Ring Transporter"
3 fingers lateral to the 4th sacral spinous process and slightly inferior, on the fourth sacral foramen. Anal Sphincter Shu point.

Anuria, Constipation, Toxicity

At the bottom of the lower sacrum the meridian zigs up to 2 fingers lateral to the spinous process and slightly inferiorly on the sacrum for points Bl 31 through Bl 34.

Bl 31 上髎 Shangliao "Upper Bone Hole"
2 fingers lateral to the first sacral spinous process, inside of Bl 27.

Anuria, Constipation, Genital Problems, Mucous Discharge, Periods Painful.

Bl 32 次髎 Ciliao "Second Bone Hole"
2 fingers lateral to the second sacral spinous process, inside of Bl 28.

Anuria, Constipation, Genital Problems, Mucous Discharge, Periods Painful.

Bl 33 中髎 Zhongliao "Middle Bone Hole"
2 fingers lateral to the third sacral spinous process, inside of Bl 29.

Anuria, Constipation, Genital Problems, Mucous Discharge, Periods Painful.

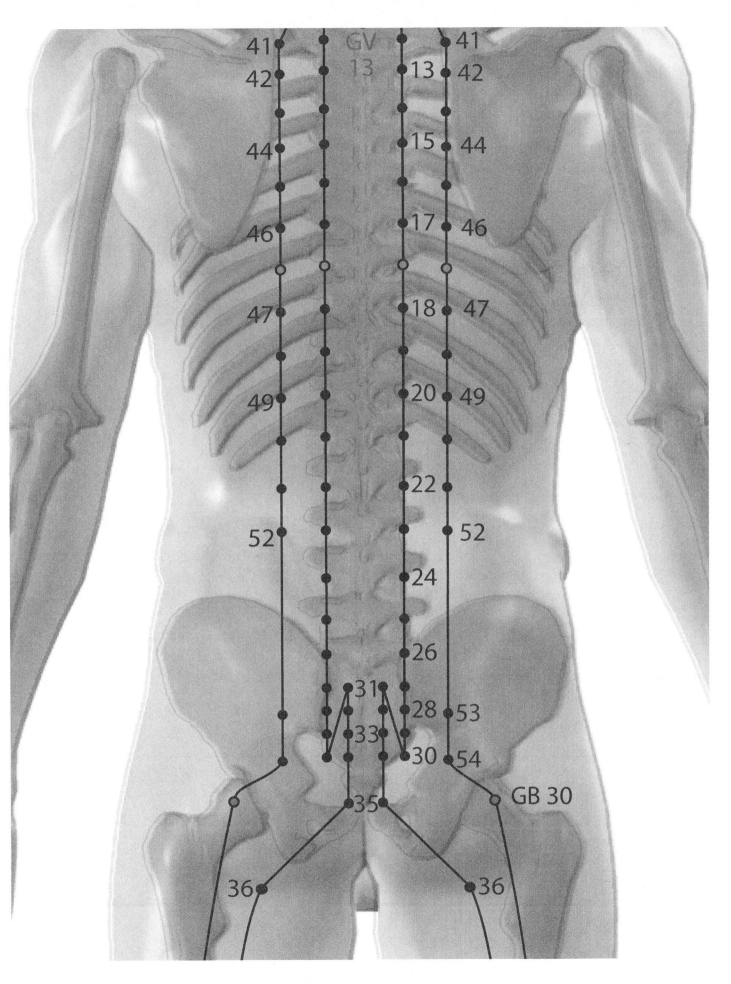

Bladder Meridian

Bl 34 下髎 Xialiao "Lower Bone Hole"

2 fingers lateral to the fourth sacral spinous process, inside of Bl 30.

Anuria, Constipation, Genital Problems, Mucous Discharge, Periods Painful.

Bl 35 會陽 Huiyang "Meeting of Yang"

2 fingers lateral to the base of the coccyx.

Intestinal Inflammation, Mucous Discharge.

Bl 36 承扶 Chengfu "Hold and Support"

Inferior to the ischial tuberosity (sitz bone) in the gluteal fold at the bottom of the buttock.

Neck Spasm, Upper Lung Inflammation.

Bl 37 殷門 Yinmen "Hamstring Gate"

Eight fingers inferiorto Bl 36 in the center of the hamstring.

Inflammation in a line like a cable through this area on Bladder Meridian is an indication of sciatic nerve problems.

Breathing Difficulty, Bronchitis, Heart Problems.

Bl 38 浮郄 Fuxi "Superficial Cleft"

2 fingers superior to Bl 39.

Bronchitis, Depression, Memory Poor, Pulmonary Tuberculosis, Weakness.

Bl 39 委陽 Weiyang "Lateral End of the Crease"

2 fingers lateral to Bl 40, just to the inside of the tendon.

Breathing Difficulty, Bronchitis, Heart Problems.

Bl 40 委中 Weizhong "Middle of the Crease"

Located in the center of the back of the knee joint. With the knee bent at a 45 degree angle, insert your finger into the bend in the back of the knee in the center. Keep your finger there and straighten the knee, you'll find you're on the swelling below the hollow. Bl 40 is on the swelling, not in the hollow.

Anorexia, Insomnia, Nervous Problems, Night Sweats, Pericarditis, Weakness.

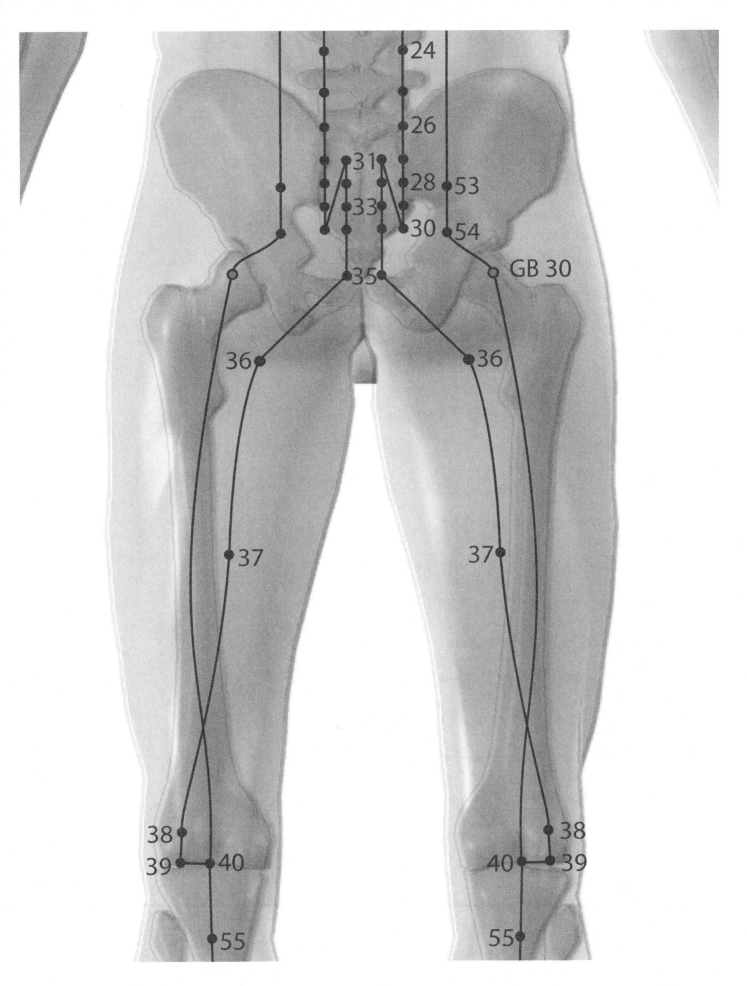

From here, the meridian numbering resumes at the outer bladder meridian at the top of the back, just outside of the vertical band of the erector spinae.

Bl 41 附分 Fufen "Outer Branch"

3 fingers lateral to Bl 12, four fingers outside of the bottom the spinous process of the second thoracic vertebra, just outside of the vertical band of the erector spinae.

Anorexia, Diaphragm Problems, Intestinal Inflammation.

Bl 42 魄戶 Pohu "Door of the Corporeal Soul"

3 fingers lateral to Bl 13.

Anorexia, Chest Problems, Digestive Problems, Liver Abscess, Rheumatism, Shock.

Bl 43 膏肓俞 Gaohuangshu "Vital Region Shu"

3 fingers lateral to Bl 14.

Anorexia, Digestive Problems, Laziness, Liver Problems, Rheumatism, Chest Problems.

Bl 44 神堂 Shentang "Spirit Hall"

3 fingers lateral to Bl 15.

Anorexia, Digestive Problems, Liver Problems, Rheumatism, Chest Problems.

Bl 45 譩譆 Yixi "That Hurt"

3 fingers lateral to Bl 16.

Abdominal Distension, Coldness, Edema, Stomach Problems, .

Bl 46 膈關 Geguan "Diaphragm Gate"

3 fingers lateral to Bl 17.

Constipation (Chronic), Breast Inflammation, Endocrine Problems.⊠

Bl 47 魂門 Hunmen "Ethereal Soul Gate"

3 fingers lateral to Bl 18.

Genital Problems, Kidney Problems.

Bl 48 陽綱 Yanggang "Linking to Gall Bladder"

3 fingers lateral to Bl 19.

Anuria, Back Pain, Constipation, Intestinal Inflammation.

Bl 49 意舍 Yishe "Abode of Thought"

3 fingers lateral to Bl 20.

Bladder Infection, Hemorrhoids.

Bl 50 胃倉 Weicang "Stomach Granary"

3 fingers lateral to Bl 21.

Anal Inflammation, Anuria, Constipation, Hip Problems.

Bl 51 肓門 Huangmen "Vitals Gate"

3 fingers lateral to Bl 22 bottom of ribs.

Back Pain, Hip Problems, Leg Pain.

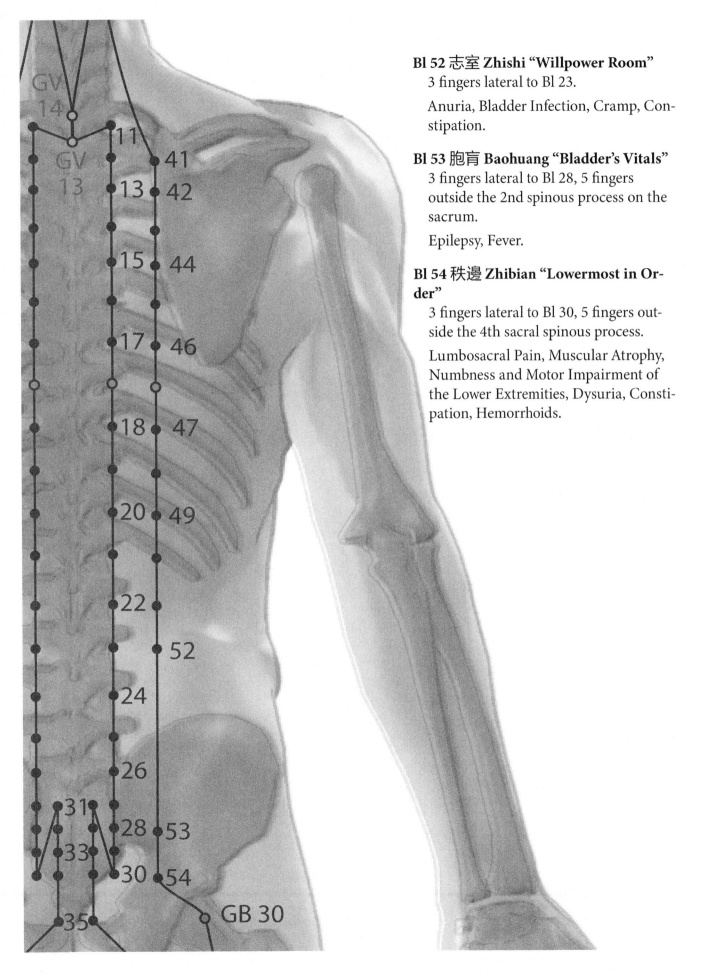

Bl 52 志室 Zhishi "Willpower Room"

3 fingers lateral to Bl 23.

Anuria, Bladder Infection, Cramp, Constipation.

Bl 53 胞肓 Baohuang "Bladder's Vitals"

3 fingers lateral to Bl 28, 5 fingers outside the 2nd spinous process on the sacrum.

Epilepsy, Fever.

Bl 54 秩邊 Zhibian "Lowermost in Order"

3 fingers lateral to Bl 30, 5 fingers outside the 4th sacral spinous process.

Lumbosacral Pain, Muscular Atrophy, Numbness and Motor Impairment of the Lower Extremities, Dysuria, Constipation, Hemorrhoids.

From here the meridian intersects with GB 30 and then meets the other branch of the Bladder Meridian at Bl 40.

Bl 55 合陽 Heyang "Yang Confluence"

3 fingers inferior to Bl 40.

Back Pain, Swollen Glands, Uterine Hemorrhage.

Bl 56 承筋 Chengjin "Sinews Support"

4 fingers inferior to Bl 55.

Constipation, Cramping.

Bl 57 承山 Chengshan "Mountain Support"

4 fingers inferior to Bl 56..

Constipation, Cramping.

Bl 58 飛陽 Feiyang "Taking Flight"

Diagonally 3 fingers laterally and inferiorly from Bl 57.

Epilepsy.

Bl 59 跗陽 Fuyang "Tarsus Yang"

4 fingers inferior to Bl 58, 5 fingers superior to Bl 60.

Chronic Conditions.

Bl 60 昆侖; 崑崙 Kunlun "Kunlun Mountains"

From the peak of the lateral malleolus (the ankle bump), move posteriorly into the depression between the malleolus and the Achilles tendon.

Birthing Difficult, Glandular Diseases.

Bl 61 僕參 Pucan "Subservient Visitor"

Halfway between the peak of the lateral malleolus and the corner of the heel in a slight depression, or 2 fingers inferior and 2 fingers posterior to Bl 62.

Knee Arthritis, Epilepsy, Shock.

Bl 62 申脈 Shenmai "Extending Vessel"

Directly inferior to the lateral malleolus.

Stroke.

Bl 63 金門 Jinmen "Golden Gate"

Halfway between Bl 62 & Bl 64.

Epilepsy, Shock.

Bl 64 京骨 Jinggu "Metatarsal Tuberosity"

On the proximal lateral edge of the 5th metatarsal where the shaft of the bone meets the proximal head.

Cerebral Congestion, Epilepsy, Fever, Heart Problems, Meningitis.

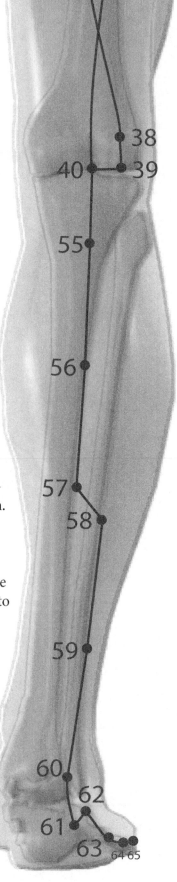

Bl 65 束骨 Shugu "Metatarsal Head"

On the distal lateral edge of the 5th metatarsal where the shaft of the bone meets the distal head.

Boils, Cancerous Ulcers.

Bl 66 足通谷 Zutonggu "Foot Valley Passage"

Located at the lateral side of the pinky toe the proximal knuckle where shaft meets knuckle, where the side and top of the toe meet.

Stomach Inflammation, Uterine Congestion.

Bl 67 至陰 Zhiyin "Reaching Yin"

Located at the lateral base of the pinky toenail.

Anuria, Foot Arthritis, Labor Difficult, Paralysis.

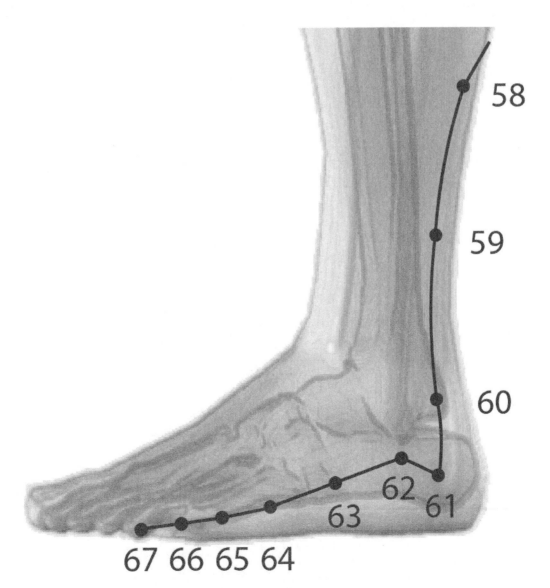

Bladder Meridian

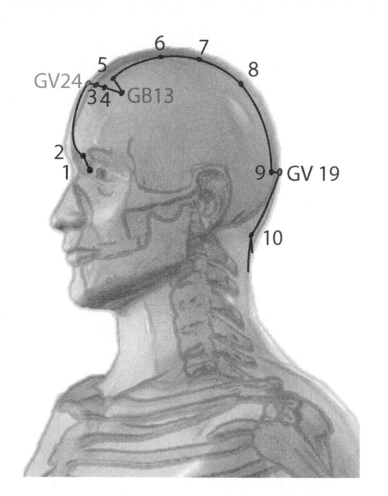

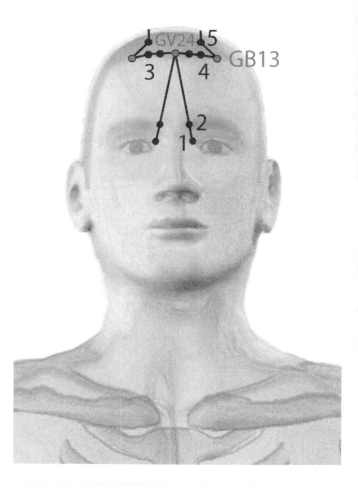

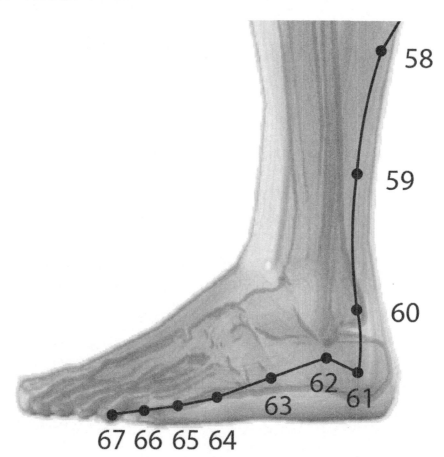

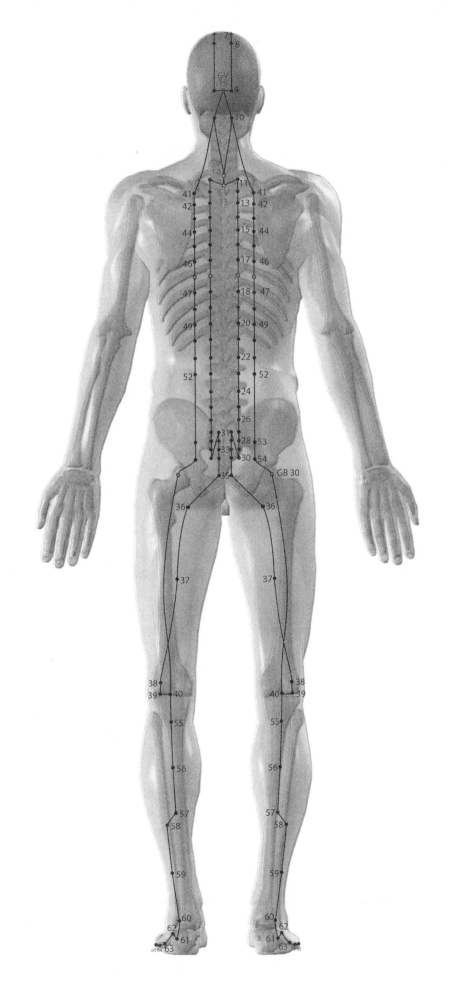

Bladder Meridian

足少陰腎經
Kidney Meridian
of Foot Shao Yin (Lesser Yin)

Primary Balancing and Five Element Points

Wood/Sedation	Ki 1	Well
Fire	Ki 2	Spring
Source/Earth	Ki 3	Stream
Metal/Tonification	Ki 7	River
Water/Horary	Ki 10	Sea
Luo	Ki 4	
Accumulation/Xi Cleft	Ki 5	

Key Attributes of the Kidney Meridian

Element: Water
Season: Winter
Stage of Life: Storage
Climate: Cold
Sense Organ: Hearing
Tissue Governed: Bones, Hair on Head

Emotions: Fear, Anxiety
Balanced Attributes: Courage
Yang Organ: Bladder
Time: 5-7 pm
Color: Black/Blue
Flavor: Salty

Common Physical Symptoms of Imbalance:

Bones Ache, Weak
Cold Extremities (Especially the feet).
Darkness Under Eyes
Drowsiness, Lack of Energy
Diarrhea (Also Spleen, Liver, Large Intestine)
Dizziness on Standing (Rush)
Ears Ring (Tinnitus)
Edema
Foolhardy

Hearing Loss
Low Back Pain
Menstruation Irregular (Also Liver)
Premenstrual Syndrome (Also Liver)
Reproductive Problems
Soles of Feet Painful, Hot
Urinary Incontinence
Sexual or Reproductive Problems
Hypertension (Also Liver Or Spleen)
Hair Loss

Common Emotional Symptoms of Imbalance:

Fear, Easily frightened
Chronic Anxiety

About the Kidney Meridian

The kidneys are paired organs found in the middle back. They are about twelve centimeters long and weigh approximately 15 kilograms each.

The kidneys maintain the fluid balance in the body; filter poisons from the blood (such as uric acid); regulate substances in the blood that we need for health (such as sodium and other electrolytes); convert vitamin D into a usable hormone; and maintain the body's acid-alkaline balance. The kidneys excrete water and waste products through the creation of urine, which passes to the bladder via the ureter tubes. While the kidneys are essential to life, it's quite possible to survive with only one.

In Chinese medicine, the Kidney system is responsible for the energy of the body and is considered the root of life and vitality. It controls the Jing Qi, or essential energy of the body which activates bodily and cellular processes and maintains the health, vitality, and function of every organ, system, and sense. Kidney deficiency, or a deficiency of Jing, manifests as low energy, inability to fully mature, premature aging, or senility.

Kidneys also governs the bones and the hair on the head (the last things to decay when we die), the reproductive organs, and our inner ear and hearing.

Kidney Yin and Kidney Yang - while every Organ has a Yin and a Yang aspect, this is especially important in relation to the Kidney system. You can think of these functions as energy moving into storage (Yin) and moving out of storage into the body (Yang). If Kidney Yin is less than Kidney Yang, the person's energy will deplete and lead to deficiency symptoms. If Kidney Yang is less than Kidney Yin, there will not be enough energy circulating in the body leading to lack of function and stagnation symptoms such as weight gain and edema.

Kidney Meridian Point Index

Ki 1 涌泉 Yong Quan "Bubbling Well"

On the underside of the foot between the 2nd and 3rd metatarsal bones in the soft spot just posterior to the pad of the forefoot.

Shock Recovery/Revival, Anxiety, Cough, Dizziness, Epilepsy, Female Sterility, Heart Problems, Headache, Jaundice, Meningitis, Throat Sore, Tonsillitis, Urinary Blockage.

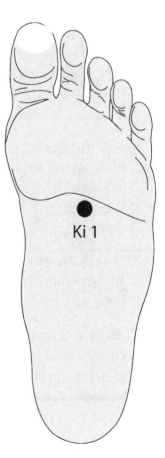

Ki 2 然谷 Rangu "Blazing Valley"

In the medial arch, in the belly of the abductor hallucis just inferior to the niche where the 1st cuneiform and the navicular bones meet.

Bladder Infection, Convulsions (Children), Diabetes, Heart Inflammation, Periods Painful, Pharyngitis, Sperm Insufficient, Testes Inflamed, Uterine Congestion, Tonsillitis, Vaginal Itch.

Ki 3 太谿 Taixi "Great Stream"

In the groove halfway between the peak of the medial malleolus and the Achilles tendon. You'll feel a little bead there.

Anorexia, Breathing Difficult, Cold Extremities, Constipation, Cough, Endocarditis, Insomnia.

Ki 4 大鐘 Dazhong "Large Bell"

2 fingers inferior to Ki 3 and slightly posterior, pressing down into the superior aspect of the calcaneus.

Anxiety, Constipation, Mucous Discharge, Psychopathy, Uterine Spasm.

Ki 5 水泉 Shuiquan "Water Spring"

Halfway between the peak of the medial malleolus and the corner of the heel in a slight depression.

Menstrual Problems, Urinary Problems.

Ki 6 照海 Zhaohai "Shining Sea"

Just inferior to the medial malleolus.

Epilepsy, Erection Involuntary, Fatigue in Limbs, Hernia, Insomnia, Mucous Discharge, Painful Period, Psychopathy, Tonsillitis, Throat Dry.

Ki 7 復溜 Fuliu "Continuing Flow"

2 fingers posterior to Ki 8.

All Kidney Problems, Abdominal Distention or Inflammation, Arteries Swollen, Cold Feet, Cold in Bones, Edema, Flatulence, Hemorrhoids (Bleeding), Jaundice, Marrow Inflamed, Paraplegia, Saliva Excessive, Toothache, Urinary or Bladder Infection.

Ki 8 交信 Jiaoxin "Intersecting with Spleen"

From Sp 6 (6 fingers above the peak of the medial malleolus on the edge of the tibia), 2 fingers posterior and 2 fingers inferior.

Constipation, Intestinal Inflammation, Marrow Inflamed, Menstruation Excessive, Mucous Discharge, Periods Painful, Urinary Blockage.

Ki 9 築賓 Zhubin "Strong Knees"

3 fingers superior to Sp 6 and 4 fingers posterior to the tibia in the lower gastrocnemius.

Dementia, Chronic Conditions, Poisoning, Psychopathy.

Ki 10 陰谷 Yingu "Yin Valley"

On the medial side of the back of the knee joint, 3 fingers medially from Bl 40, opposite Bl 39.

Abdominal Distension, Knee Arthritis, Menstruation Excessive, Mucous Discharge, Penis Pain, Vaginal Infection.

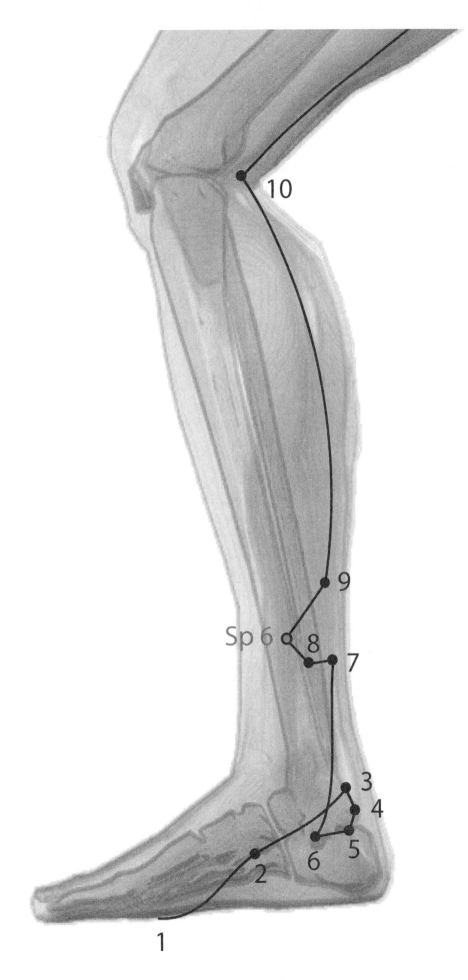

Sp 6

Kidney Meridian

Ki 11 橫骨 Henggu "Pubic Bone"

On the superior edge of the pubic bone, halfway between the center (pubic symphysis) and superior angle of the bone.

Eye Congestion or Inflammation, Hernia, Male Sterility, Mucous Discharge, Semen Leakage.

Ki 12-21 are each 2 fingers from the median line; 3 fingers between the left and right.

Ki 12 大赫 Dahe "Big Plentifulness"

2 fingers superior to Ki 11.

Eye Congestion or Inflammation, Male Sterility, Penis Pain, Sperm Insufficient, Vaginal Infection (Chronic).

Ki 13 氣穴 Qixue "Kidney Qi Cave"

2 fingers superior to Ki 12.

Back Pain or Spasm, Eye Congestion or Inflammation, Kidney Inflammation, Male Sterility, Semen Leakage.

Ki 14 四滿 Siman "Fourth for Fullnesses"

2 fingers superior to Ki 13.

Hernia, Intestinal Inflammation, Uterine Spasm, Vision Obscured.

Ki 15 中注 Zhongzhu "Pouring into the Middle"

2 fingers superior to Ki 14.

Constipation, Eustachian Tube Inflammation, Eye Congestion or Inflammation, Fallopian Inflammation, Intestinal Inflammation, Period Painful.

Ki 16 肓俞 Huangshu "Vitals Tissues Shu"

3 fingers outside of navel, 2 fingers superior to Ki 15.

Constipation (Chronic), Diarrhea, Eye Congestion or Inflammation, Hernia, Jaundice.

Ki 17 商曲 Shangqu "Metal Bend"

3 fingers superior to Ki 16.

Anorexia, Eye Congestion or Inflammation, Hernia, Jaundice.

Ki 18 石關 Shiguan "Stone Gate"

2 fingers superior to Ki 17.

Anorexia, Constipation, Eye Congestion, Mucous Discharge, Salivation Excessive, Uterine Congestion, Uterine Spasm.

Ki 19 陰都 Yindu "Yin Metropolis"

2 fingers superior to Ki 18.

Breathing Difficulty, Eye Congestion, Flatulence, Hernia, Pulmonary Emphysema, Vision Problems.

Ki 20 腹通谷 Futonggu "Abdominal Food Passage"

2 fingerS superior to Ki 19.

Breathing Difficulty, Digestion Poor, Eye Congestion, Stomach Inflamed, Pulmonary Emphysema, Weakness.

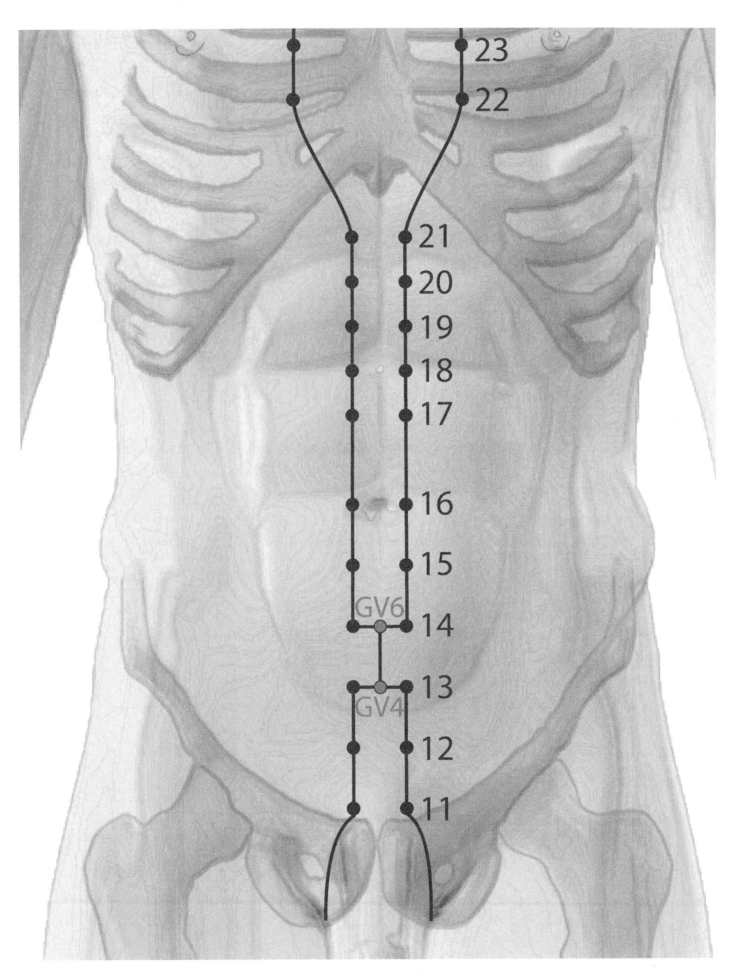

23
22
21
20
19
18
17
16
15
GV6
14
13
GV4
12
11

Ki 21 幽門 Youmen "Hidden Gate"

2 fingers superior to Ki 20, just below the rib cage in the niche where the 6th and 7th ribs meet. The most superior you can fit 3 fingers laterally.

Bronchitis, Liver Problems, Morning Sickness, Swallowing Painful.

Ki 22 步廊 Bulang "Stepping Upwards"

Located in the 5th intercostal space between the 5th and 6th ribs, 4 fingers lateral to the midline.

Anorexia, Bronchitis, Nose Problems.

Ki 23 神封 Shenfeng "Spirit Manor"

3 fingers superior to Ki 22 in the 4th intercostal space (between 4th and 5th ribs), 4 fingers lateral to the midline.

Anorexia, Breast Tumor, Bronchitis, Nose Problems.

Ki 24 靈墟 Lingxu "Spirit Ruin"

3 fingers above Ki 23 in the 3rd intercostal space (between 3rd and 4th ribs), 4 fingers lateral to the midline.

Anorexia, Breast Inflammation, Breast Tumor, Bronchitis, Nose Problems.

Ki 25 神藏 Shencang "Spirit Storehouse"

3 fingers above Ki 24 in the 2nd intercostal space (between 2nd and 3rd ribs), 4 fingers lateral to the midline.

Anorexia, Breathing Stopped or Difficult, Bronchitis.

Ki 26 彧中 Yuzhong "Refined Chest"

3 fingers above Ki 25 in the 1st intercostal space (between 1st and 2nd ribs), 4 fingers lateral to the midline.

Anorexia, Bronchitis.

Ki 27 俞府 Shufu "Shu Mansion"

From the head of the medial end of the clavicle, 4 fingers lateral to the midline.

Anorexia, Asthma, Breathing Stopped, Bronchitis.

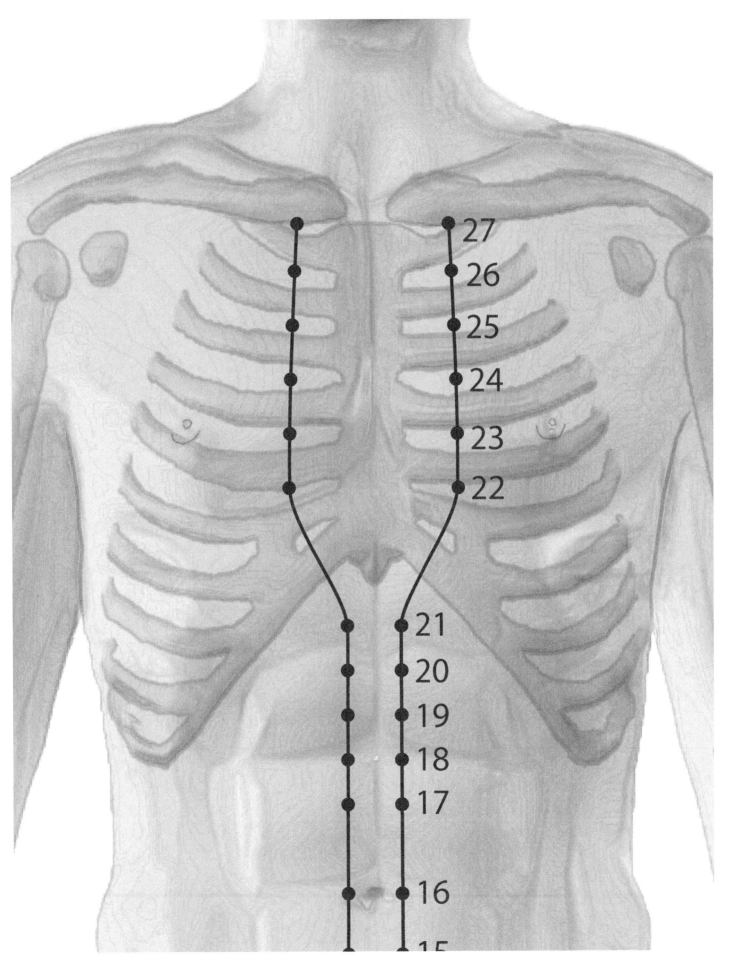

Kidney Meridian

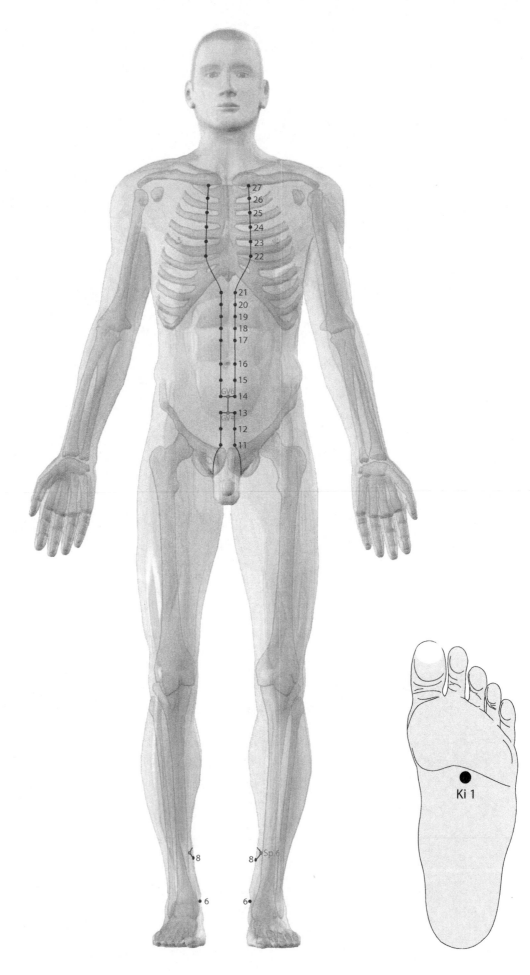

Integrative Acupressure Meridian Atlas

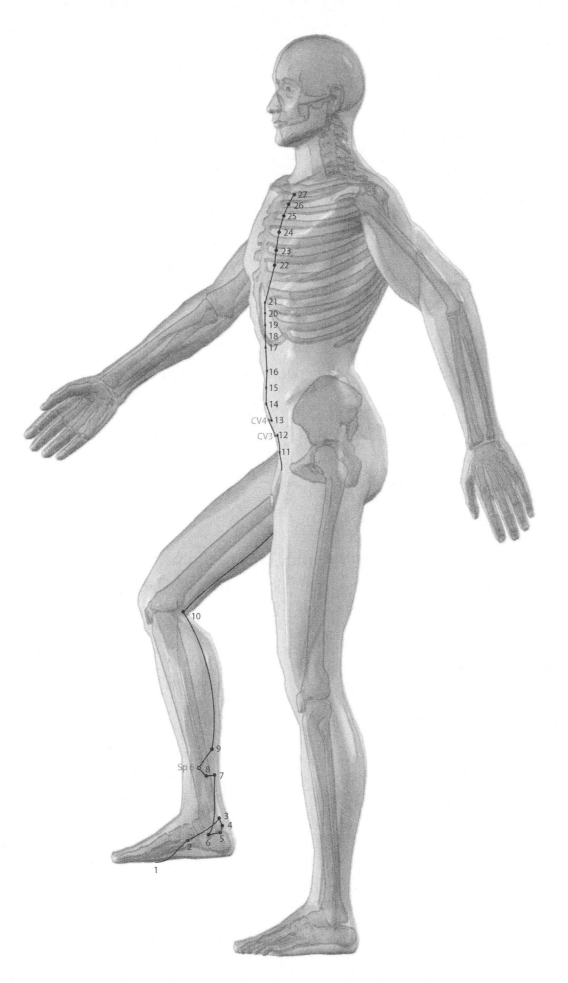

Kidney Meridian

手厥陰心包經
Pericardium Meridian
of Hand Jue Yin (Faint Yin)

Primary Balancing and Five Element Points

Wood/Tonification	Pc 9	Well
Fire/Horary	Pc 8	Spring
Earth/Source/Sedation	Pc 7	Stream
Metal	Pc 5	River
Water	Pc 3	Sea
Luo	Pc 6	
Accumulation/Xi Cleft	Pc 4	

Key Attributes of the Pericardium Meridian

Element: Fire
Season: Summer
Stage of Life: Growth
Climate: Hot
Sense Organ: Tongue
Tissue Governed: Blood

Emotions: Love, Sexual Excitement
Balanced Attribute: Quiet Joy
Yang Organ: Triple Warmer
Time: 7-9 pm
Color: Purple Red
Flavor: Spicy, Bitter

Common Physical Symptoms of Imbalance:

Arm and Elbow Stiffness or Spasm
Chest and Ribs Distended
Face Red
Discomfort in Chest
Excessive Laughter
Palms Hot

Sexual Dysfunction
Underarm Painful or Swollen
Upper Chest Tension
Vision Blurred
Head and Neck Painful, Stiff

Common Emotional Symptoms of Imbalance:

Depression
Feeling and Expressing Emotions Difficult
 Phobias

About the Pericardium Meridian

The word pericardium is derived from Latin Peri (around) and Cardium (heart). In Western physiology, the pericardium is a tough fibrous sack surrounding the heart. It protects the heart from physical damage and from friction, since the heart is constantly moving.

Western medicine does not consider the pericardium to be an organ, whereas in Chinese medicine it is. Chinese Medicine considers the Pericardium meridian to function in a similar, albeit more expanded, way. Other names for this meridian are the Heart Protector and the Circulation/Sex/Pericardium meridian which names its three major functions - regulating the circulation of Blood through and around the Heart, generating sexual attraction, and protecting the Heart both physically and from the effects of strong emotions.

As the pericardium physically protects the heart, the Pericardium meridian absorbs Heat and protects the heart from attacks of fever. Most of the points on the meridian reduce Heat symptoms associated with Heart or Blood ailments, and the last three are used for high fevers and sunstroke.

Because of its close ties to the Heart, the Pericardium Meridian is often used to treat mental/emotional disorders, as well as to engender joy and happiness, to communicate our emotions, and protect the heart from emotional stress. It does this by calming the mind and balancing the emotions. In addition, it is strongly linked with sexual intimacy, moderating the raw sexual energy of the Kidneys with the love generated by the Heart.

The Pericardium meridian is coupled with the Triple Warmer meridian.

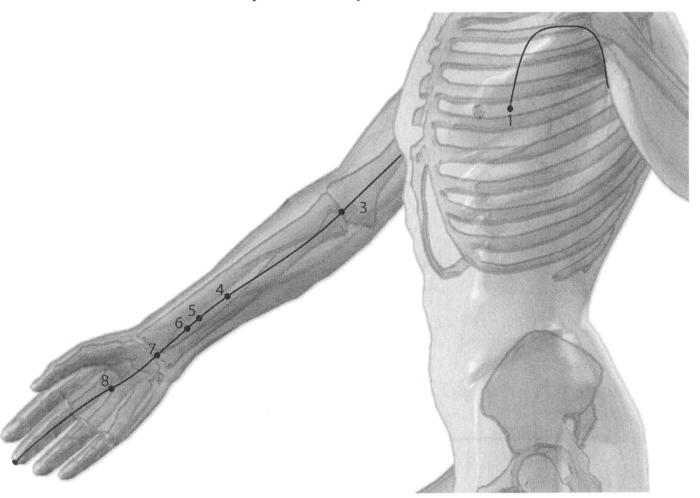

Pericardium Meridian Point Index

Pc 1 天池 Tianchi "Heavenly Pool"

Starting at the front of the armpit onto the torso, move inferiorly 3 fingers to between the 4th and 5th ribs.

Breast Inflammation, Cerebral Congestion, Cerebral Anemia, Gland Inflammation (Under Arm), Lactation Insufficient, Pericarditis.

Pc 2 天泉 Tianquan "Heavenly Spring"

Starting at the front of the armpit onto the upper arm, 4 fingers down on the interior groove of the biceps.

Anorexia, Anxiety, Bronchitis, Endocarditis, Eyesight Problems, Flatulence, Pulmonary Congestion, Vomiting.

Pc 3 曲澤 Quze "Marsh at the Crook"

In the center of the crease of the elbow joint.

Bronchitis, Female Sterility, Myocarditis, Vomiting.

Pc 4 郄門 Ximen "Xi-Cleft Gate"

3 fingers proximal from Pc 5.

Cough (Chronic), Myocarditis, Nosebleed, Psychopathy, Vomiting Blood.

Pc 5 間使 Jianshi "Intermediate Messenger"

2 fingers proximal from Pc 6.

Epilepsy, Heart Inflammation, Nervous Problems, Nightmare, Periods Painful, Stomach Pain, Stroke, Throat Sore, Uterine Congestion, Womb Inflammation.

Pc 6 內關 Neiguan "Inner Pass"

4 fingers proximal from Pc 7.

Emotional Problems, Menstrual Irregularity, Psychological Problems, Elbow Pain, Endocarditis, Eye Hemorrhage, Hiccups, Jaundice, Myocarditis, Stomach Pain.

Pc 7 大陵 Daling "Great Mound"

In the center of the crease of the wrist joint pressing into the junction of the heads of the radius and ulna and the lunate bone.

Endocarditis, Epilepsy, Fever, Glands Swollen, Headache, Insomnia (Mental Activity Excessive), Intercostal Pain, Myocarditis, Stomach Pain, Stomach Bleeding, Tonsillitis.

Pc 8 勞宮 Laogong "Palace of Toil"

In the center of the palm, the space between the 3rd and 4th metacarpal.

Arteriosclerosis, Epilepsy, Gum or Mouth Inflammation, Jaundice, Nosebleed.

Pc 9 中衝 Zhongchong "Middle Rushing"

Located at the tip of the middle finger.

Cerebral Congestion, Cerebral Anemia, Fever (No sweat), Myocarditis, Stroke.

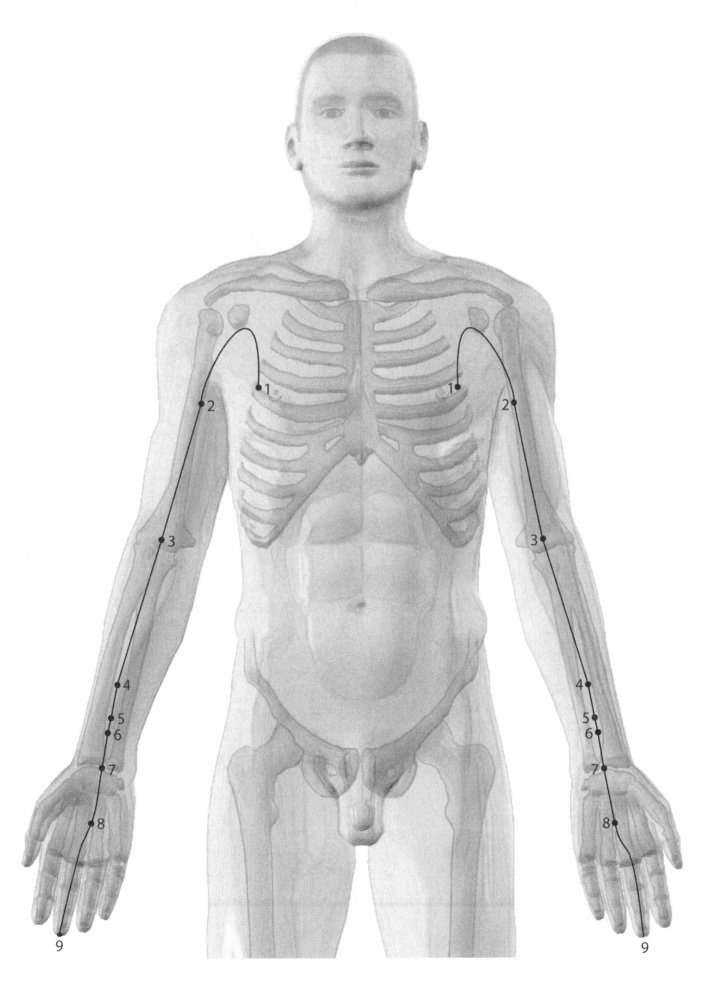

Pericardium Meridian

手少陽三焦經
Triple Warmer Meridian
of Hand Shao Yang (Lesser Yang)

Primary Balancing and Five Element Points

Metal	TW 1	Well
Water	TW 2	Spring
Wood/Tonification	TW 3	Stream
Fire/Horary	TW 6	River
Earth/Sedation	TW 10	Sea
Source	TW 4	
Luo	TW 5	
Accumulation/Xi Cleft	TW 7	

Key Attributes of the Triple Warmer Meridian

Element: Fire	Emotions: Love, Sexual Excitement
Season: Summer	Balanced Attribute: Quiet Joy
Stage of Life: Growth	Yang Organ: Triple Warmer
Climate: Hot	Time: 9-11 pm
Sense Organ: Tongue	Color: Purple Red
Tissue Governed: Blood	Flavor: Spicy, Bitter

Common Physical Symptoms of Imbalance:

Abdomen Distended, Full	Eye Pain In Outer Corner
Colds & Fevers	Jaw Swollen
Confusion	Perspiration When Sleeping Or For No Reason
Deafness and/or Pain Behind Ear	Slow Metabolism, Overweight
Elbow Problems	Fast Metabolism, Hyperactive

Common Emotional Symptoms of Imbalance:

Addictions	Depression
Anxiety	Feeling overwhelmed

About the Triple Warmer Intestine Meridian

The Triple Warmer, or San Jiao, also known as the "Three Burners", "Triple Burner" or "Triple Heater," does not correlate with a specific organ and therefore has no Western version, but rather is seen as a function that balances the circulation of Qi, Blood, Fluids, and hormones (hypothalamus and endocrine system). It is central in maintaining the body's metabolism.

The Triple Warmer derives its name from "three parts that burn," or three centers of activity, within the body. The upper burner is associated with the thorax including the heart and the lungs and therefore the intake of air, food and fluids. It is also involved in the distribution of protective energy (Wei Qi) on the body's exterior.

The middle burner is associated with the liver, spleen, pancreas and stomach. It is responsible for extracting energy from food and fluids and distributing it to the lungs and throughout the body.

The lower burner with the kidneys and bladder, and the large and small intestines. It is responsible for separating the pure from the impure products of digestion, absorbing nutrients and eliminating wastes. It also regulates sexual and reproductive functions.

You can also think of the Triple Warmer as balancing the overall functions of intake, transformation, and elimination both on a whole body level and on the cellular level. While many different Organ meridians are involved in these functions, the Triple Warmer acts to organize and coordinate between all of these physically, and as well emotionally and mentally.

Triple Warmer Meridian Point Index

TW 1 關衝 Guanchong "Surge Gate"
The medial base (corner) of the nail on the fourth (ring) finger.

Anorexia, Dry Heaves, Film over Eyes, Headache, Stroke.

TW 2 液門 Yemen "Fluid Gate"
Proximal end of the proximal phalange of the fourth finger where the shaft meets the knuckle, posterior to the attachment of the web.

Anemic Headache, Deafness, Dizziness, Film over Eyes, Gums Inflamed.

TW 3 中渚 Zhongzhu "Central Islet"
Distal end of the fourth metatarsal where the shaft meets the head, pressing into the shaft, head and tissue.

Arthritis (Arm), Deafness, Dizziness, Film over Eyes, Headache, Pharynx Inflamed.

TW 4 陽池 Yangchi "Yang Pool"
In the center of the crease of the wrist on dorsal arm, pressing between the heads of the radius and ulna and the lunate.

Arthritis (Wrist), Coldness, Diabetes, Fever (Intermittent), Rheumatism.

TW 5 外關 Waiguan "Outer Pass"
4 fingers proximal to TW 4, between the radius and the ulna.

Arthritis (Arm), Deafness, Eye Problems, Toothache.

TW 6 支溝 Zhigou "Branch Ditch"
2 fingers proximal to TW 5.

Bronchial Pneumonia, Chest Congestion (Pleurisy), Constipation (Chronic), Fever (After Chilled), Myocarditis, Vomiting.

TW 7 會宗 Huizong "Convergence and Gathering"
2 fingers lateral to TW 6.

Arm Lacks Strength, Chronic Glandular Problems, Epilepsy.

TW 8 三陽絡 Sanyangluo "Three Yang Connection"
2 fingers proximal to TW 6 between the radius and the ulna.

Arm Lacks Strength, Deafness, Eye Problems, Fatigue, Lower Teeth Pain.

TW 9 四瀆 Sidu "Four Rivers"
5 fingers proximal to TW 8 between the radius and the ulna.

Deafness, Kidney Inflammation, Lower Teeth Pain, Nasal Inflammation.

TW 10 天井 Tianjing "Upper Well"
With the arm straight, just superior to the olecranon process (point of the elbow).

Bronchitis, Cough, Deafness, Depression, Eye Inflammation, Insanity, Lumbar Pain, Nasal Inflammation, Nervous Exhaustion, Stroke, Tonsillitis.

TW 11 清冷淵 Qinglengyuan "Cooling Deep Pool"
4 fingers proximal to TW 10 on the humerus.

Arm Spasm, Shoulder Problems.

TW 12 消濼 Xiaoluo "Draining Marsh"
5 fingers proximal to TW 11 on the humerus between the deltoid and triceps muscles.

Epilepsy, Headache, Rheumatism, Shoulder Spasm, Swollen Glands (Neck).

TW 13 臑會 Naohui "Upper Arm Intersection"
5 fingers proximal to TW 12, on back of the V formed by the attachment of the deltoid muscle.

Neck Inflamed, Shoulder Spasm.

TW 14 肩髎 Jianliao "Shoulder Bone Hole"
Inferior to the distal scapula spine just to the outside of the tendon.

Chest Infection (Pleurisy), Shoulder Spasm.

TW 15 天髎 Tianliao "Upper Arm Hole"
Just superior to the superior medial angle of the scapula.

All Conditions Brought About by Cold or Damp Weather, Neck Cold, Sweat Absent.

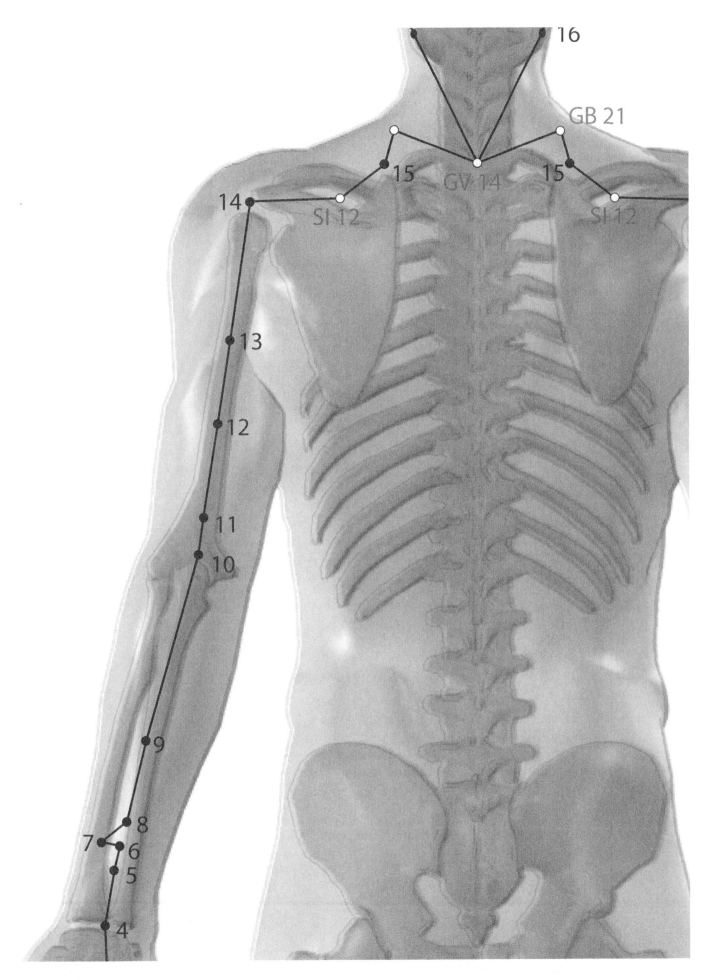

Triple Warmer Meridian

TW 16 天牖 Tianyou "Sky Window"

4 fingers inferior and 2 fingers posterior to TW 17. Just behind the SCM (sternocleidomastoid muscle).

Deafness, Eye Congestion, Water Retention.

TW 17 翳風 Yifeng "Wind Screen"

Just inferior to the ear lobe and posterior to the jaw.

Deafness, Ears Ring, Jaw Inflamed, Mumps, Muteness, Swollen Glands (Jaw).

From here, the meridian traces around the edge of the ear on the skull.

TW 18 契脈 Qimai["Convulsion Vessel"

3 fingers diagonally superiorly and posteriorly from TW 17, tracing around the ear on the skull.

Cerebral Congestion, Deafness, Diarrhea, Ears Ring, Headache, Vomiting.

TW 19 顱息 Luxi "Head's Tranquility"

2 fingers superiorly from TW 18, tracing around the ear on the skull.

Breathing Difficult, Cerebral Congestion, Deafness, Ear Infection, Ears Ring, Epilepsy, Headache, Vomiting (Children).

TW 20 角孫 Jiaosun "Angle Vertex"

Just superior to the top of the ear on the edge of the hairline.

Chewing Difficult, Eyes Bulge, Film over Eyes, Lip Contraction, Vomiting.

TW 21 耳門 Ermen "Ear Gate"

Just anterior to the tragus (ear flap) and just inferior to the zygomatic arch. When opening the jaw fully, there will be an indent here caused by the head of the mandible moving anteriorly.

Ear Infection, Ears Ring, Lip Contraction, Upper Teeth Pain.

TW 22 耳和髎 Erheliao "Ear Harmonising Foramen"

3 fingers superior to TW 21 and just superior to the zygomatic arch.

Ears Ring, Headache, Nasal Inflammation or Polyps, Swollen Lymph Glands.

TW 23 絲竹空 Sizhukong "Silken Bamboo Hollow"

On the lateral side edge of the eyebrow in a small niche at the anterior edge of the temple.

Dizziness, Eye Congestion, Eye Problems, Film over Eyes, Headache.

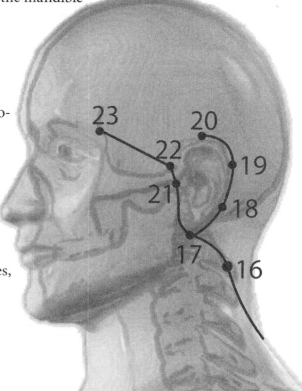

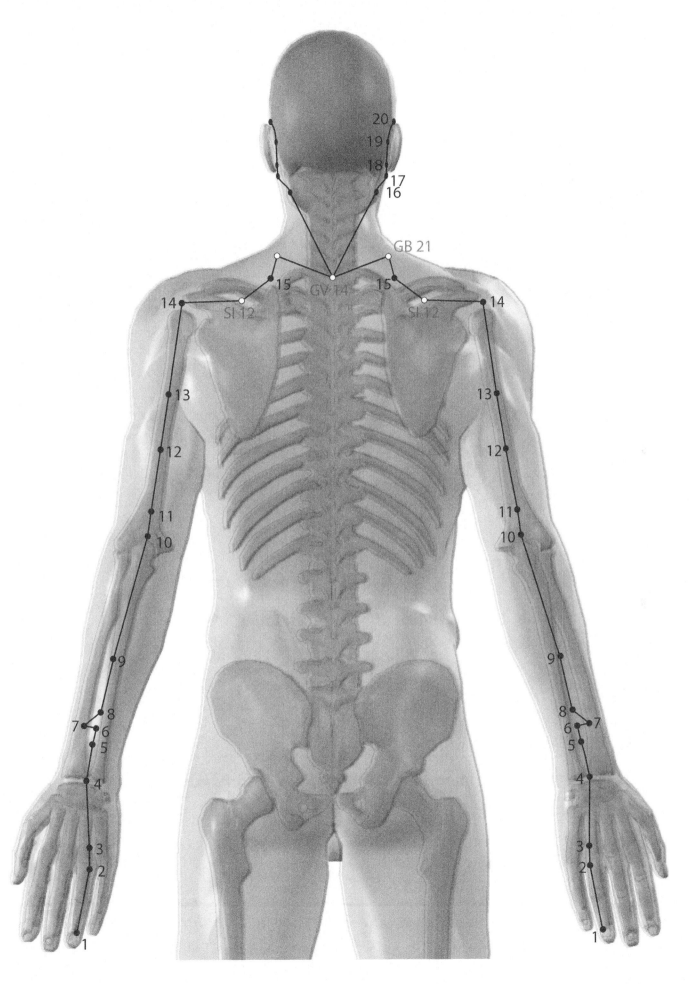

20
19
18
17
16

GB 21

15   15
SI 12   GV 14   SI 12

14   14

13   13

12   12

11   11
10   10

9   9

8   8
7   6   6   7
5   5

4   4

3   3
2   2

1   1

Triple Warmer Meridian

足少陽膽經
Gall Bladder Meridian
of Foot Shao Yang (Lesser Yang)

Primary Balancing and Five Element Points

Metal	GB 44	Well
Water/Tonification	GB 43	Spring
Wood/Horary	GB 41	Stream
Fire/Sedation	GB 38	River
Earth	GB 34	Sea
Source	GB 40	
Luo	GB 37	
Accumulation/Xi Cleft	GB 36	

Key Attributes of the Gall Bladder Meridian

Element: Wood

Season: Spring

Stage of Life: Creation

Climate: Windy

Sense Organ: Sight

Tissue Governed: Tendons, Ligaments

Emotions: Anger, Frustration

Balanced Attributes: Will Power, Creativity

Yin Organ: Liver

Time: 11pm - 1am

Color: Green

Flavor: Sour

Common Physical Symptoms of Imbalance:

Headaches in Temple

Ear and Eye Pain (Especially Outer Corner of Eye)

Joint Stiffness and Pain

Side of Chest Tightness/Pain (Ribs)

Nausea and Vomiting

Eyes Yellow

Headaches (Migraines Included)

Stiffness in Fourth Toe

Gall Stones

Common Emotional Symptoms of Imbalance:

Anger, Frustration (Excess Qi)

Depression, Lack of Will (Deficient Qi)

About the Gall Bladder Meridian

The gallbladder is a small muscular pouch under the liver that takes the liquid bile acids and cholesterol created by the liver and draws the water out of it to concentrate it, then secretes the bile into the duodenum to aid in digestion. Bile acids emulsify and assist in the digestion of the fats we eat; at the same time, they keep the cholesterol within the gallbladder from forming stones. For its part, cholesterol buffers the bile acids and keeps them from irritating the organ.

The liver creates bile in an ongoing process and passes it to the gallbladder through the hepatic duct and the cystic duct. Once the gallbladder concentrates the bile, as needed its muscles tighten and push the bile out the cystic duct and down the common bile duct to the duodenum.

In Chinese medicine, the Gall Bladder is known traditionally as the "upright official who excels through their decisions and judgment;" the Gall Bladder is said to play an essential role in each person's ability to make sound decisions. Good judgment and clear thinking are made possible, when the Gall Bladder is balanced. When the Organ is in disharmony, however, anger and frustration (excess) or lack of motivation and depression (deficiency) dominate and decision-making is clouded.

The Gall Bladder is seen as an external manifestation of the Liver energy. Thus, Liver symptoms and signs become more pronounced when the Gall Bladder is imbalanced. Anger, for example, can become explosive and verbal, and illnesses related to both the Liver and Gall Bladder will be acute and inflamed.

Gall Bladder Meridian Point Index

GB 1 瞳子髎 Tongziliao "Pupil Crevice"
Located at the outer corner of the eye orbit, just onto the flat area of the zygomatic bone.

Eye Problems, Eyesight Poor, Facial Spasms, Migraine.

GB 2 聽會 Tinghui "Meeting of Hearing"
Just anterior to where the bottom of the earlobe attaches to the head, in a little niche on the posterior edge of the mandible.

Deafness, Ear Infection, Ears Ring, Lockjaw, Toothache.

GB 3 上關 Shangguan "Above the Joint"
On the superior edge of the zygomatic arch, 3 fingers anterior to the ear.

Deafness, Dizziness, Ears Ring, Glaucoma, Stroke.

GB 4-7—best to start from GB 8 and work backward.

GB 4 頷厭 Hanyan "Jaw Serenity"
2 fingers superior to GB 5 (3 fingers above the center of the ear and 5 fingers forward). Also 2 fingers lateral and 2 fingers inferior to St 8.

Convulsions (Children), Dizziness, Ears Ring, Headache, Mucous Excessive, Toothache.

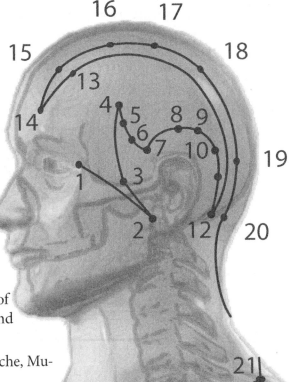

GB 5 懸顱 Xuanlu "Suspended Skull"

2 fingers diagonally superiorly and anteriorly from GB 6.

Brain Weakness, Facial Congestion, Headache, Mucous Excessive, Toothache.

GB 6 懸厘 Xuanli "Suspended Hair"

2 fingers diagonally superiorly and anteriorly from GB 7.

Brain Weakness, Fever (Sweatless), Mucous Excessive, Toothache.

GB 7 曲鬢 Qubin "Crook of the Temple"

3 fingers anterior and 2 fingers inferior to GB 8.

Eye Problems, Neck Pain.

GB 8 through 12 are 3 fingers from the closest aspect of the outer helix of the ear.

GB 8 率谷 Shuaigu "Leading Valley"

2 fingers superior to the top of the helix of the ear (2 fingers superior to TW 20).

Eye Problems, Cough, Drunkenness, Thirst Excessive, Headache.

GB 9 天沖 Tianchong "Heavenly Rushing"

2 tight fingers posterior and slightly inferior to GB 8.

Epilepsy, Headache, Mouth Inflamed, Muscle Cramp (Violent).

GB 10 浮白 Fubai "Floating White"

diagonally 3 fingers posterior and inferior to GB 9.

Breathing Problems, Cough (Chronic), Deafness, Ears Ring, Tonsillitis, Toothache.

GB 11 頭竅陰 Touqiaoyin "Yin Portals of the Head"

2 fingers inferiorly from GB 10. Or starting at the most inferior aspect of the posterior of the mastoid bone along the occipitomastoid suture (where the SCM attaces), move superiorly until just before you move onto the occipital bone. Also 2 fingers superior to GB 12.

Cancer, Cough (Chronic), Deafness, Meningitis.

GB 12 完骨 Wangu "Mastoid Process"

At the bottom of the mastoid, behind where the SCM attaches, move just posterior and superior into the niche where the occiput meets the mastoid (bottom of the occipitomastoid suture).

Ear Infection, Eye Muscle Problems, Insomnia, Mouth Inflamed, Muteness, Tonsillitis.

GB 13 本神 Benshen "Root of the Spirit"

2 fingers lateral from GB 15 at the hairline.

Epilepsy, Dizziness, Headache.

GB 14 陽白 Yangbai "Yang White"

Starting at the eyebrow above the center of the eye, locate the point In the depression of the forehead 1/2 way from the eyebrow to the hairline,.

Eye Problems, Facial Spasm, Headache.

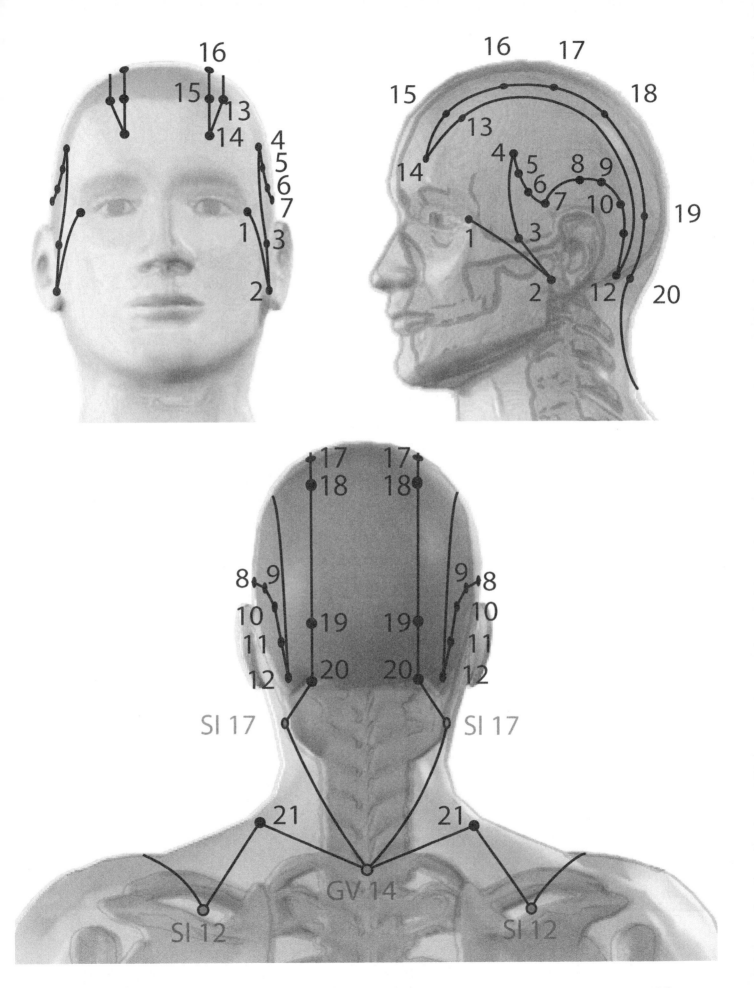

Gall Bladder Meridian

GB 15 頭臨泣 Toulinqi "Head Governor of Tears"

Located 3 fingers superior to GB 14 at the hairline.

Epilepsy, Eyes Water Excessively, Stroke.

GB 16 目窗 Muchuang "Window of the Eye"

Located 4 fingers posterior to GB 15.

Abscess, Dizziness, Eyesight Weak, Fever (From Cold Exposure), Headache.

GB 17 正營 Zhengying "Upright Nutrition"

Located 3 fingers posterior to GB 16.

Dizziness, Eyesight Weak, Headache, Toothache.

GB 18 承靈 Chengling "Support Spirit"

Located 4 fingers posterior to GB 17.

Breathing Difficult, Coldness, Fever, Headache, Nosebleed.

GB 19 腦空 Naokong "Brain Hollow"

Located 4 fingers superior to GB 20.

Anxiety, Breathing Difficult, Coldness, Fever, Headache, Nosebleed.

GB 20 風池 Fengchi "Wind Pool"

Located on the lateral edge of the attachment of the trapezius to the occiput, or 4 fingers from the midline, at the base of the skull.

Special Point for All Brain Disorders.
Ear, Eye or Nose Problems, Ears Ring, Headache, Stroke.

GB 21 肩井 Jianjing "Shoulder Well"

Located at the most superior aspect of the shoulder, 2 fingers from the base of the neck.

Brain Weakness, Breast Inflammation, Neck & Shoulder Muscle Problems, Uterine Hemorrhage.

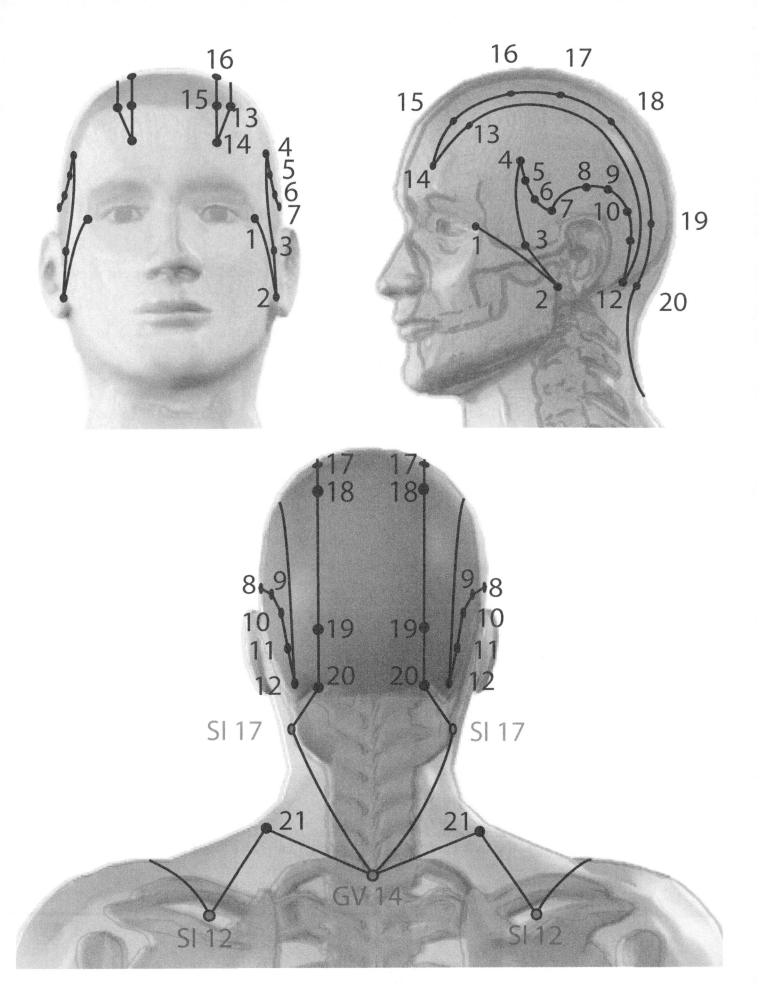

Gall Bladder Meridian

GB 22 淵腋 Yuanye "Armpit Abyss"

With the arm raised, directly below the center of the armpit (Ht 1) 4 fingers, between the 4th and 5th ribs.

Fever (From Cold), Pleurisy.

GB 23 輒筋 Zhejin "Flank Sinews"

2 fingers anterior to GB 22 between the 4th and 5th ribs.

Abdomen (Lower) Inflammation, Depression, Saliva Excessive, Speech Problems.

GB 24 日月 Riyue "Sun and Moon"

On the line running vertically through the nipple, between the 7th and 8th ribs (the lowest intercostal space on that line) 8 fingers laterally from the midline.

Depression, Hernia, Jaundice, Liver Problems, Stomach & Abdomen Problems.

GB 25 京門 Jingmen "Capital Gate"

Starting at the side of the body just below the rib cage, move posteriorly 2 fingers to just lateral to the end of the 12th rib.

Abdominal Pain, Colic, Flatulence, Hypertension, Kidney Inflammation.

GB 26 帶脈 Daimai "Girdling Vessel"

On the side of the body halfway between the ileum and the ribcage (11th rib).

Fever (From Cold), Periods Painful, Uterine Pain, Womb Inflammation.

GB 27 五樞 Wushu "Five Pivots"

2 fingers medial to the ASIS (anterior superior iliac spine, the point at the top front of the hip bone).

Constipation, Hernia, Testicle Inflammation, Urinary Problems, Uterine Pain, Womb Inflammation.

GB 28 維道 Weidao "Linking Path"

Inferiorly 2 fingers from GB 27.

Abdominal Swelling, Anorexia, Cecum Inflamed, Colitis, Kidney Inflammation, Testicle Inflammation, Uterine Problems, Womb Inflammation.

GB 29 居髎 Juliao "Stationary Crevice"

Just superior to the greater trochanter of the femur (where you feel the hip bone on the side of the hip).

Bladder Inflammation, Cecum Inflammation, Kidney Inflammation, Periods Painful, Testicle Inflammation, Uterine Problems, Vaginal Discharge.

GB 30 環跳 Huantiao "Jumping Circle"

1/3 of the distance from the greater trochanter to the ischial tuberosity (the sharp bone that you sit on).

Knee Pain, Lumbar Pain, Paralysis (One Side).

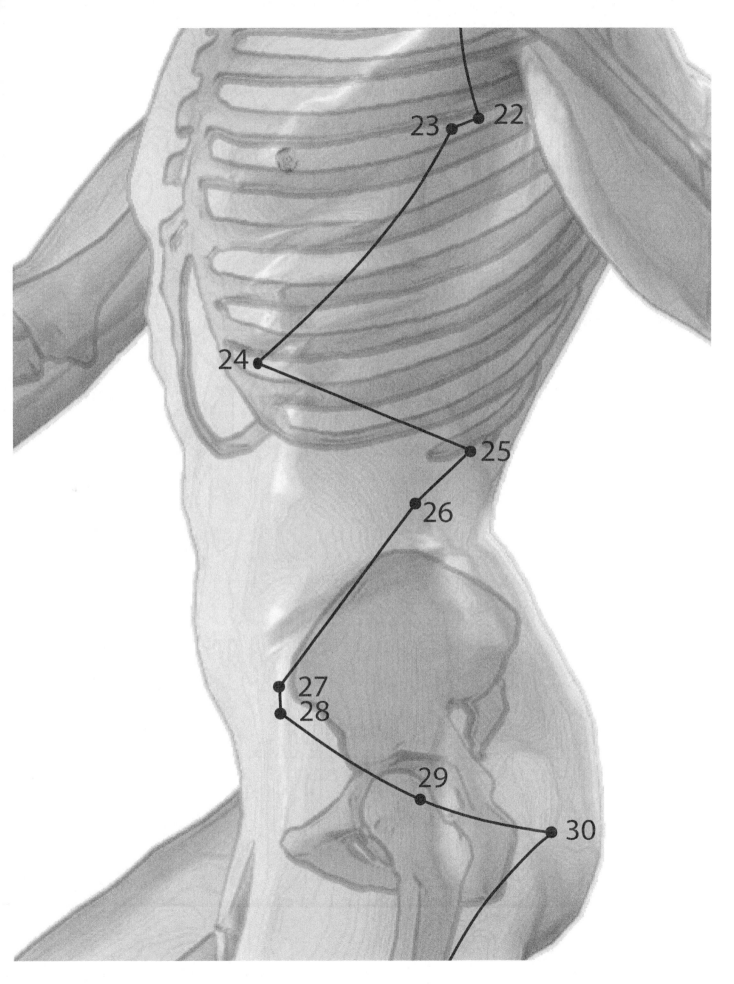

GB 31 風市 Fengshi "Wind Market"

Standing with your arms at your sides, where the proximal joint of the middle finger touches the leg. Feel around for the sore spot.

Leg Spasm.

GB 32 中瀆 Zhongdu "Middle Ditch"

3 fingers inferior to GB 31.

Special Point for Paralysis (One Side).
Muscle Spasm.

GB 33 膝陽關 Xiyangguan "Knee Yang Gate"

Where the shaft and head of the femur meet, just posterior to attachment of the iliotibial band, press into the femur.

Special Point for Pain.

Rheumatism.

GB 34 陽陵泉 Yanglingquan "Yang Mound Spring"

Anterior to the head of the fibula, inferior to where the fibula and tibia meet.

Special Point for Muscle Spasms.

General Tonic, Vitality, Resistance to Disease, Arteriosclerosis, Chronic Constipation.

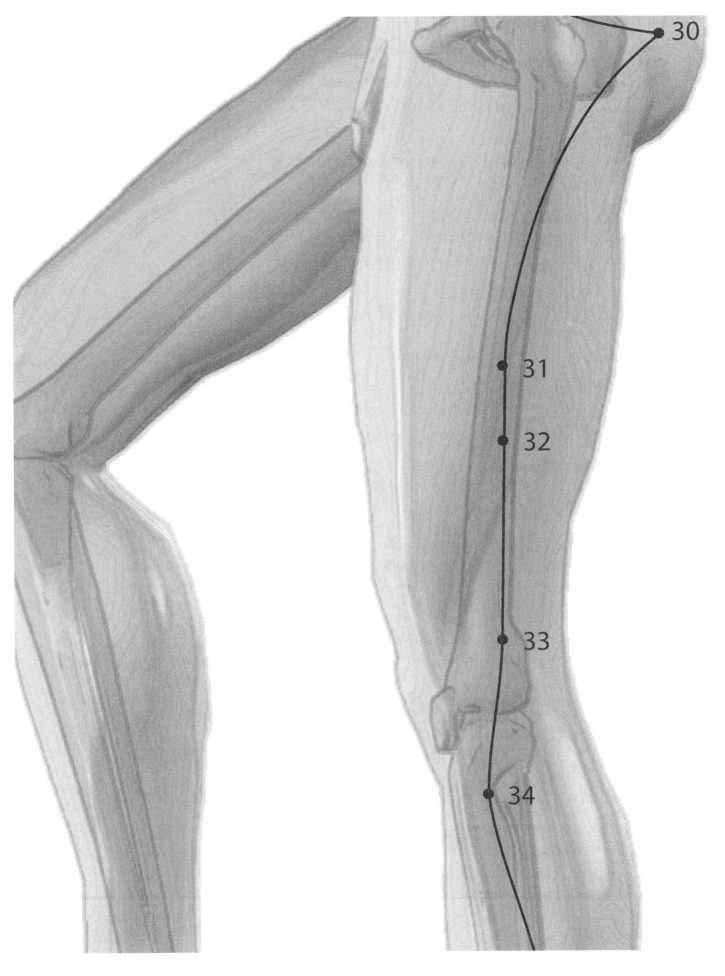

Gall Bladder Meridian

GB 35 陽交 Yangjiao "Yang Intersection"

Posteriorly from GB 36 2 fingers, on the posterior edge of the fibula. Also 2 fingers anterior to Bl 58.

Breathing Difficult, Chest Inflammation, Legs Weak.

GB 36 外丘 Waiqiu "Outer Hill"

Superiorly 3 fingers from GB 37 on the lateral edge of the fibula.

Chest Inflammation, Epilepsy, Legs Weak.

GB 37 光明 Guangming "Bright Light"

Superiorly 2 fingers and slightly posteriorly from GB 38.

Calf Muscle Problems, Eye Problems, Legs Weak, Teeth Grinding.

GB 38 陽輔 Yangfu "Yang Assistance"

Measure 7 fingers superiorly from the crown (most lateral aspect) of the lateral malleolus on the anterior edge of the fibula.

Lymph Swollen (Neck), Scrofula, Tonsillitis.

GB 39 懸鐘 Xuanzhong "Suspended Bell"

Measure 5 fingers superiorly from the crown (most lateral aspect) of the lateral malleolus.

Arteriosclerosis, Kidney Inflammation, Nosebleed, Stroke, Tonsillitis.

GB 40 丘墟 Qiuxu "Mound of Ruins"

2 fingers anterior to the bottom of the lateral malleolus in the depression.

Breathing Problems, Chest Inflammation, Hernia, Pulmonary Congestion.

GB 41 足臨泣 Zulinqi "Foot Governor of Tears"

On the top of the foot, the most proximal end of the space between the 4th and 5th metatarsals.

All Skin Diseases, Pain, Breathing Problems, Breast Inflammation, Dizziness, Endocarditis, Fever, Headache, Periods Painful, Scrofula.

GB 42 地五會 Diwuhui "Earth Five Meetings"

At the distal end of the 4th metatarsal, where the shaft meets the distal head where the top and side of the toe meet.

Breast Inflammation, Rheumatism.

GB 43 俠谿 Xiaxi "Clamped Stream"

At the juncture of the shaft and proximal head of the proximal phalange of the 4th toe where the top and side of the toe meet.

Breast Inflammation, Deafness, Spitting Blood.

GB 44 足竅陰 Zuqiaoyin "Yin Portals of the Foot"

At the lateral base of the 4th toenail.

Breast Tumor, Cerebral Anemia, Chest Inflammation, Cough (Chronic), Deafness, Dizziness, Eye Pain, Headache, Heart Dilation.

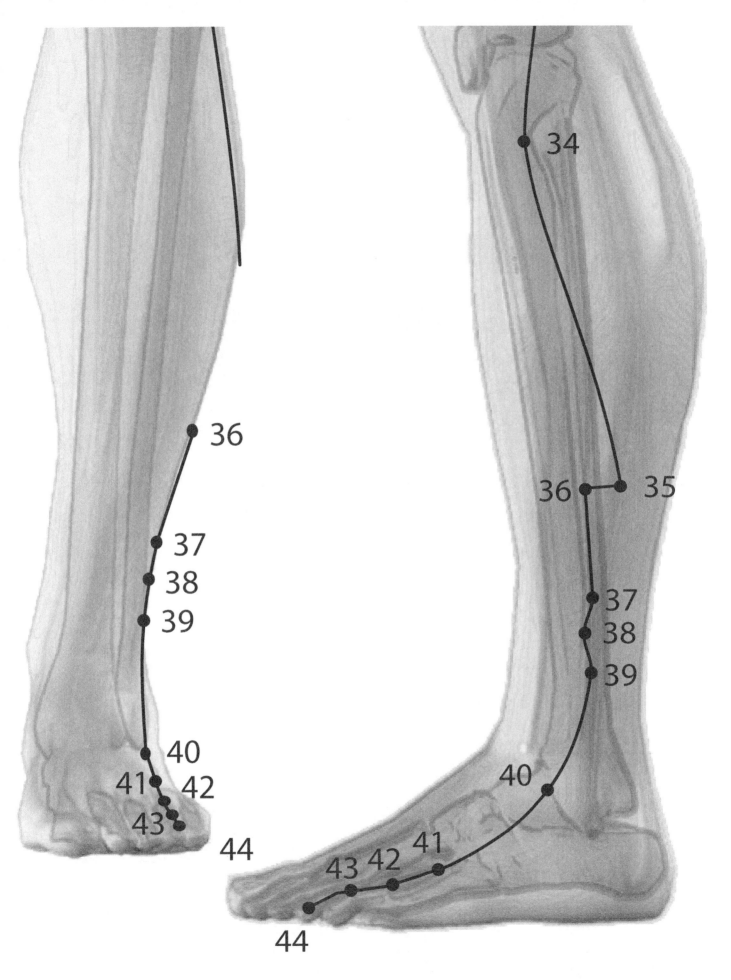

Gall Bladder Meridian

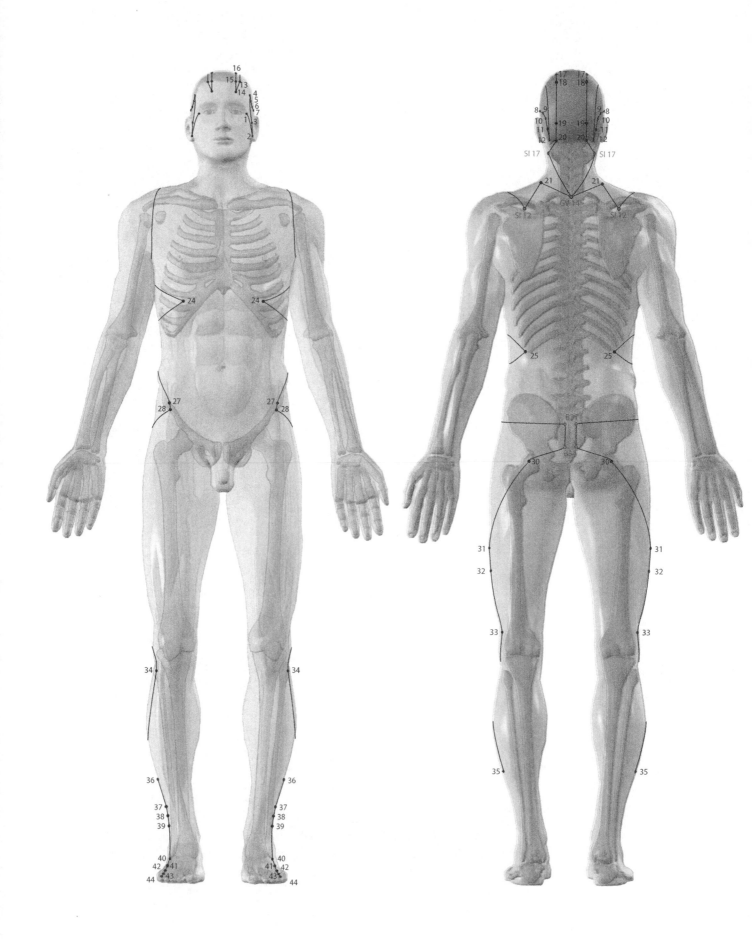

Integrative Acupressure Meridian Atlas

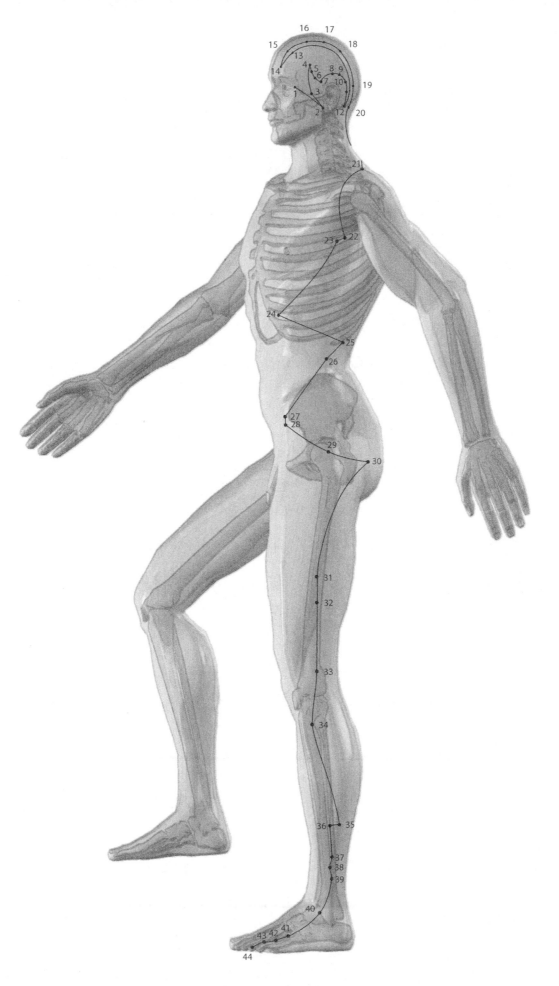

Gall Bladder Meridian

足厥陰肝經
Liver Meridian

of Foot Jue Yin (Faint Yin)

Primary Balancing and Five Element Points

Wood/Horary	Lv 1	Well
Fire/Sedation	Lv 2	Spring
Source/Earth	Lv 3	Stream
Metal	Lv 4	River
Water/Tonification	Lv 8	Sea
Luo	Lv 5	
Accumulation/Xi Cleft	Lv 6	

Key Attributes of the Liver Meridian

Element: Wood	Emotions: Anger, Frustration
Season: Spring	Balanced Attributes: Will Power, Creativity
Stage of Life: Creation	Yin Organ: Liver
Climate: Windy	Time: 11pm - 1am
Sense Organ: Sight	Color: Green
Tissue Governed: Tendons, Ligaments	Flavor: Sour

Common Physical Symptoms of Imbalance:

Red face(Excess Qi)

Pale, drawn face(Deficient Qi)

Menstrual pain, irregularity, blood clotting, PMS

Pain and swelling in genitals

Headaches at the top of the head

Migraines

Dizziness

Disorders of the eye and vision

Muscle spasms, seizures, convulsions

Pale fingernails

Tendon-related pain or disorders

Nails and cracked nails

Allergies

Easily bruised

Dandruff and hair loss

Common Emotional Symptoms of Imbalance:

Anger (Excess)

Frustration (Excess)

Depression (Deficiency)

Lack of will (Deficiency)

About the Liver Meridian

The liver is the largest of the internal organs, sitting directly under the diaphragm with its large right lobe taking up most of the lower right rib cage and smaller left lobe extending across most of the left side. It is a massively complex organ, with its main functions being detoxification; production for, and regulation of, many aspects of the body; elements of immune function; and the breakdown of fats in the digestive system through the production of bile. Functions include:

• Production of bile, which helps carry away waste and break down fats in the small intestine during digestion

• Production of certain proteins for blood plasma

• Production of cholesterol (both the "good" cholesterol, called HDL, and the "bad," or LDL) and special proteins to help carry fats through the body

• Conversion of excess glucose (blood sugar) into glycogen for storage (glycogen can later be converted back to glucose for energy) and to balance and make glucose as needed

• Regulation of blood levels of amino acids, which form the building blocks of proteins

• Processing of hemoglobin for use of its iron content (the liver stores iron)

• Conversion of poisonous ammonia to urea (urea is an end product of protein metabolism and is excreted in the urine)

• Clearing the blood of drugs and other poisonous substances

• Regulating blood clotting

• Resisting infections by making immune factors and removing bacteria from the bloodstream

• Clearance of bilirubin, also from red blood cells. If there is an accumulation of bilirubin, the skin and eyes turn yellow.

In Chinese medicine, the Liver is regarded as the "General" or "Chief of Staff" of the body because it regulates Qi flow throughout the body. Since it is the controller of the life force, the Liver is most closely associated with expression of the will, or will power, and with creativity. When life energy is weak such as in chronic depression, it very often means the Liver is troubled or weakened itself.

The Liver is associated with the eyes and sight. Any disorders of the eyes will involve the Liver. Dizziness and vertigo are also Liver related, although they can also involve the Kidney (inner ear issues) or the Spleen (excess dampness generating excess mucous). The Liver is involved with the peripheral nervous system and the tendons and ligaments, and dysfunction can manifest as muscle spasms or an inabilty to relax muscles. In addition, the Liver controls the finger- and toenails.

Liver Meridian Point Index

Lv 1 大敦 Dadun "Great and Thick"

At the lateral base of the nail of the great toe.

Constipation, Diabetes, Hernia, Lumbar Pain, Menstruation Excessive, Mucous Discharge, Penis Pain, Stomach Swollen & Cold, Urinary Incontinence.

Lv 2 行間 Xingjian "Interval Pass"

On the proximal phalange of the great toe where the shaft meets the base and where the top and side of the toe meet.

Abdominal Inflammation, Anxiety (Children), Cerebral Anemia, Colic, Constipation, Diabetes, Insomnia, Menstruation Excessive, Mouth Inflamed, Night Sweats, Pelvic Pain, Penis Pain, Toothache, Urinary Incontinence.

Lv 3 太沖 Taichong "Supreme Rush"

On the top of the foot, the most proximal end of the space between the 1st and 2nd metatarsals.

Lumbar Pain, Mucous Discharge, Uterine Hemorrhage.

Lv 4 中封 Zhongfeng "Middle Margin"

Two fingers anterior to the crown of the medial malleolus in the niche formed by the medial malleolus, the medial cuneiform bone and the bundle of tendons.

Bladder Inflammation, Jaundice, Legs Cold, Mucous Discharge.

Lv 5 蠡溝 Ligou "Gnawed Channel"

10 fingers superior to the crown of the medial malleolus (4 fingers superior to Sp 6), 2 fingers anterior to the edge of the tibia in a slight niche.

Anxiety, Colic, Periods Painful, Urinary Problems, Womb Inflammation.

Lv 6 中都 Zhongdu "Central Capital"

3 fingers superior to Lv 5.

Knee Problems, Leg Paralysis, Throat Sore.

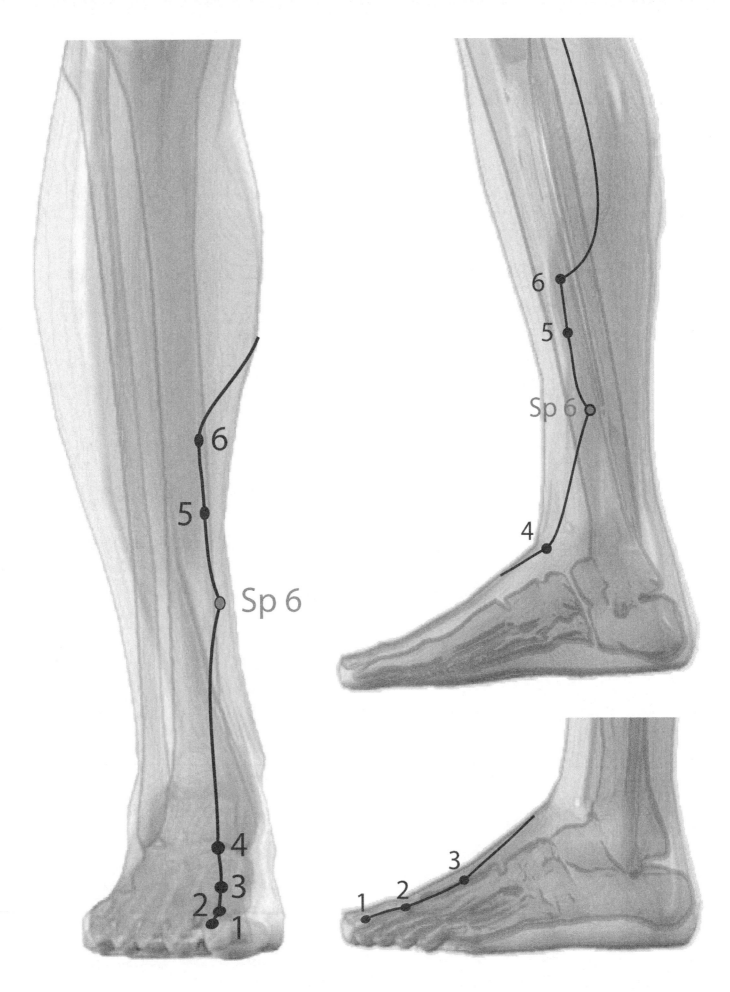

Lv 7 膝關 Xiguan "Knee Pass"

Starting where the posterior edge of the shaft of tibia meets the head (Sp 10), measure 2 fingers posteriorly.

Knee & Leg Pain.

Lv 8 曲泉 Ququan "Pool Spring"

With the knee bent 45 degrees, at the medial end of the popliteal crease just medial to the attachment point of the semimembranosus and semitendinosus muscle tendons.

Colic, Urinary Problems, Uterine Problems, Vaginal Pain or Itch.

Lv 9 陰包 Yinbao "Yin Wrapping"

7 fingers superiorly from the top of the patella, then posteriorly to between the vastus medialis (inner quadriceps) and gracilis muscles on the inside of the thigh.

Periods Painful, Urinary Problems

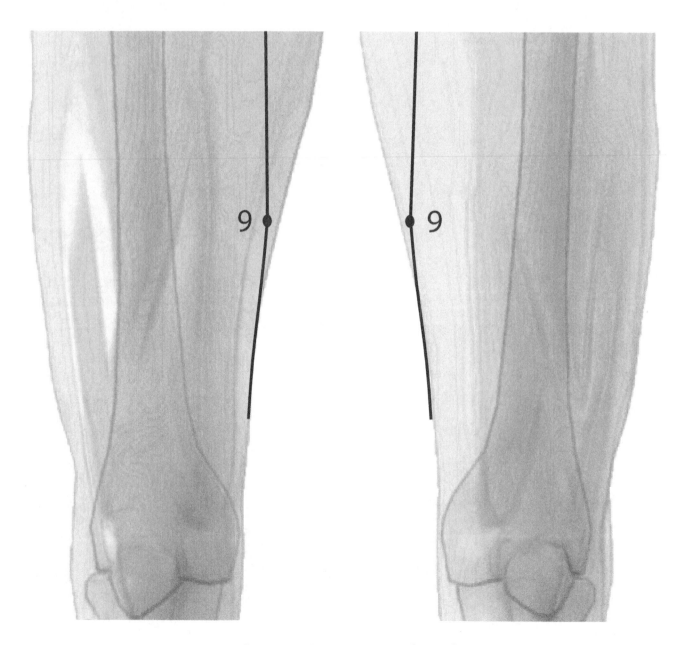

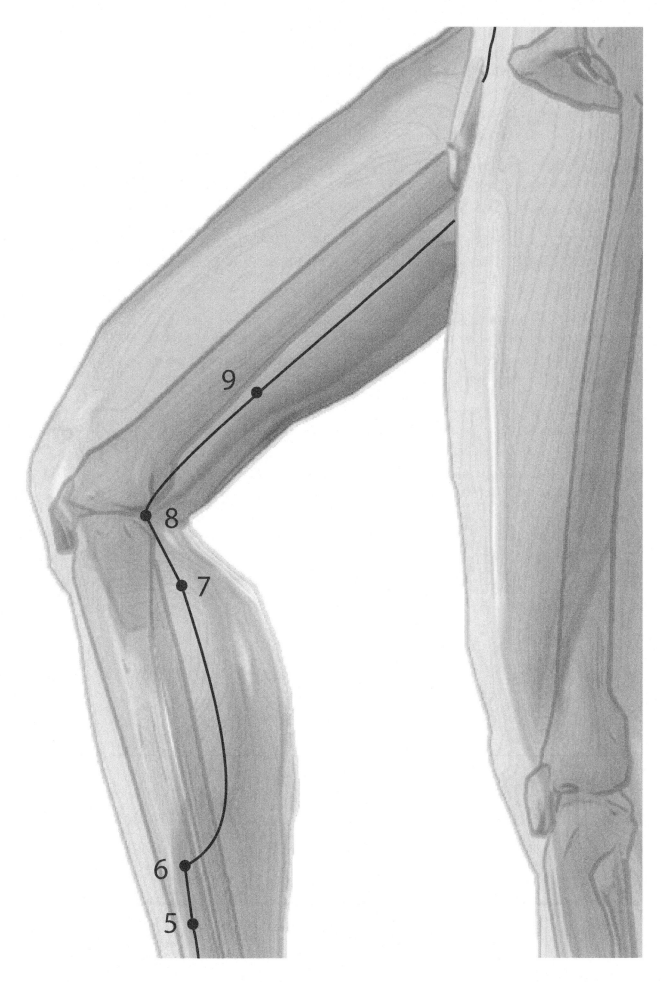

Liver Meridian

Lv 10 足五里 Zuwuli "Foot Governor of Tears"

2 fingers inferior to Lv 11.

Special Point for Insomnia

Pleurisy, Sweat Lacking, Urinary Problems, Weakness after Cold.

Lv 11 陰廉 Yinlian "Yin Side"

2 fingers inferior to Lv 12.

Vaginal Discharge or Itch.

Lv 12 急脈 Jimai "Swift Pulse"

Starting at the lateral edge of the pubic bone (St 30), measure 2 fingers inferiorly.

Hernia (Scrotal).

Lv 13 章門 Zhangmen "Gate of the Ordering"

On the side of the body just inferior to the ribs, 2 fingers anterior to the tip of the 11th (floating) rib.

Hepatitis, Jaundice, Pancreatitis, Edema, Vomiting, Indigestion, Epigastric Pain due to Food Stagnation, Diarrhea from Cold, Constipation

Lv 14 期門 Qimen "Cyclic Gate"

In the 6th intercostal space (between 6th and 7th ribs) on the mamillary line (a line drawn vertically through the nipple)..

Abdominal Inflammation, Breathing Difficult, Chest Inflammation, Cough, Hypertension, Kidney Inflammation, Vomiting after Meals.

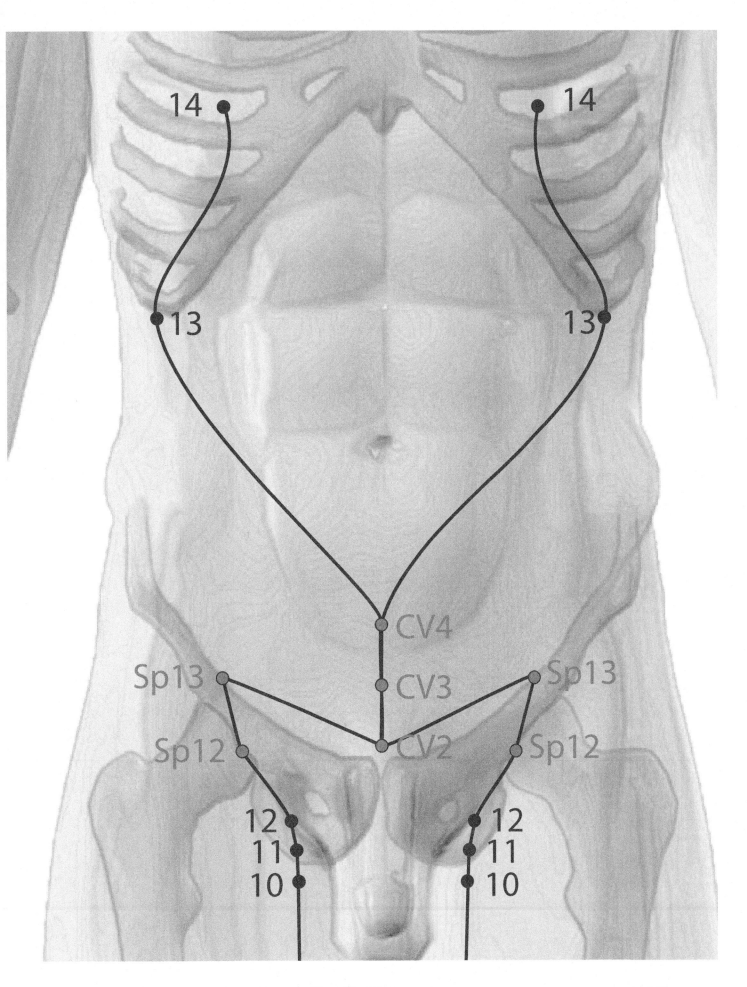

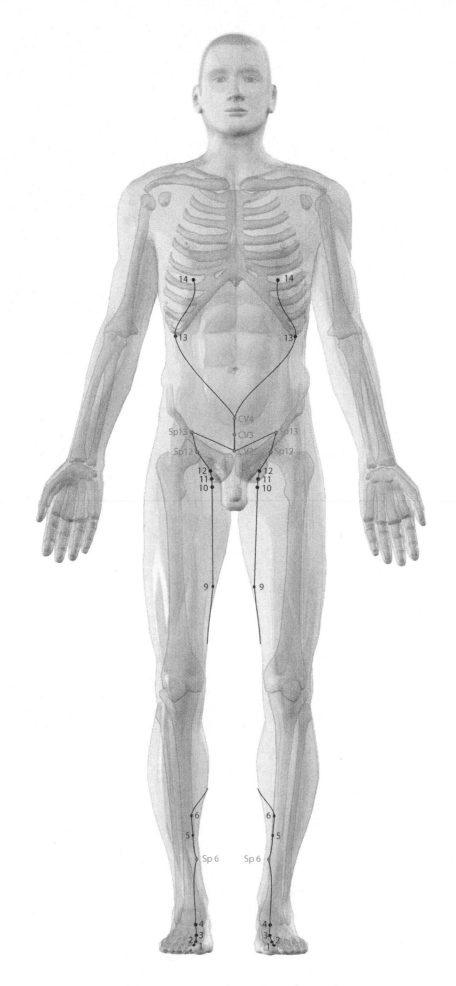

Integrative Acupressure Meridian Atlas

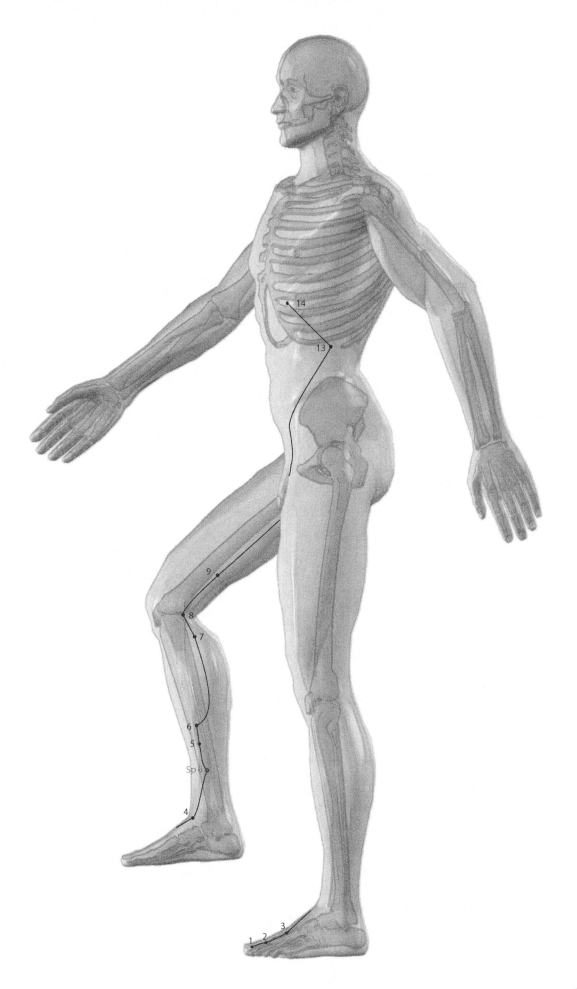

Liver Meridian

奇经八脉
The Extraordinary Meridians

The Qi Jing Ba Mai or eight "mysterious channels" help to regulate and support the Organ Meridians. They are organized into four pairs. You will see one pair on all acupuncture charts, the Conception Vessel (Du Mai) and Governing Vessel (Ren Mai), but you won't see the other three pairs on most charts. That's because they do not have points of their own, they use points of the twelve Organ meridians, weaving them together.

The Nanjing, or The Classic of Difficult Issues, one of the oldest Chinese medical texts which was compiled around the first century C.E., describes the Organ meridians as rivers and the Extraordinary Meridians as reservoirs. They act as regulators of Qi and Blood in the 12 primary meridians, absorbing excess Qi and storing it, then distributing it to areas of deficient Qi. They are very useful when there is excess in one place (for example, the shoulders and neck) and deficiency in another (the lower back and Kidneys).

The Qi Jing Ba Mai have also been called the Eight Ancestral Meridians because they help to distribute source energies stored in the Kidneys throughout the body.

The eight Extra Meridians are organized into four sets of Yin and Yang meridians. Unlike the Organ Meridians, Qi in the Extraordinary Meridians can move in either direction, moving excess Qi to areas of deficiency.

The Eight Extraordinary Meridians

The Great Central Channel - This pair consists of the Conception Vessel 任脉 (Ren Mai) which is the Yin Meridian and governs the peripheral nervous system, and the Governing Vessel 督脉 (Du Mai) which is the Yang Meridian and governs the central nervous system.

The Wei Mai 维脉 (Linking Vessels) consist of the Yin Wei Mai 陰维脉 and Yang Wei Mai 陽维脉. They function to balance the body's interior (Yin) and exterior (Yang) Qi. Its name, Wei, corresponds to the Wei Qi, the protective energy of the body related to the immune system.

The Qiao Mai 跷脉 (Heel Vessels) include the Yin Qiao Mai 陰跷脉 and Yang Qiao Mai 陽跷脉. They act to balance the upper and lower energy of the body, especially between the head/brain and the abdomen and digestive organs.

The Penetrating Vessel 冲脉 (Chong Mai) and Belt Vessel 带脉 (Dai Mai) are both related to the deep energy of the body. The Penetrating Vessel is called the Sea of Blood and is therefore very closely related to menstrual and reproductive issues. The Belt Vessel, or Girdle Vessel, acts to connect the upper and lower parts of the body especially the functioning of the legs. Long-term issues with the Belt Vessel can show as a visible disparity in size between the upper and lower body. Typically, women lean toward excess in the lower body (hips and legs) where men lean toward the upper body (beer belly and skinny legs).

Each of the eight Extra Meridians can be treated through a specific Master and Coupled point located on an Organ Meridian. The Master point acts similarly to the Source points of the Organ Meridians, balancing the Meridian. The Coupled point acts similarly to the Luo point, balancing the Meridian in relation to a paired Meridian.

Master and Coupled Points

For the **Great Central Channel**, the paired Meridians are the **Qiao Mai** so the Master point for one is the Coupled point for its Yin or Yang partner.

For the **Wei Mai**, its paired Meridians are the **Penetrating and Belt Channels** so the Master point for one is the Coupled point for its Yin or Yang partner.

For the **Qiao Mai**, the Master point of one is the Coupled point of the other.

Extra Meridians for Emotional Imbalances

The Extraordinary Meridians are often used in pairs to treat emotional imbalances. These include:

Governing Vessel and Yang Qiao Mai to treat psychosis, phobias, lack of concentration and insomnia. Points are SI 3 and Ki 6.

Belt Vessel and Yang Wei Mai to treat exhaustion, lack of motivation, depression and lethargy. Points are GB 41 and TW 5.

Conception Vessel and Yin Qiao Mai to treat chronic sadness and lack of joy, insomnia and neurosis. Points are Lu 7 and Ki 6.

Penetrating Vessel and Yin Wei Mai to treat excessive fear, phobias and anxiety, sadness, overthinking and obsessions, loss of will power, and forgetfulness. Points are Sp 4 and Pc 6.

任脉
Conception Vessel (Ren Mai)
Of the Great Central Channel

Master and Coupled Points

Conception Vessel Master   Lu 7   Conception Vessel Coupled   Ki 6

Common Physical Symptoms of Imbalance:

Asthma   Lung Problems
Coughing   Mouth Sores and Disorders
Epilepsy   Pneumonia
Eczema   Genital Disorders
Hay Fever   Itching (Deficiency)
Head & Neck Pain   Painful Abdominal Skin (Excess)
Laryngitis

Common Emotional Symptoms of Imbalance:

Anxiety   Obsessive Behavior
Insomnia   Sadness, Depression

Although it has no corresponding organ in Western medicine, the Conception Vessel is seen by the Chinese as the regulator of the peripheral nervous system, whereas its Yang partner the Governing Vessel controls the central nervous system. The Conception Vessel relates to responsibility for, or fostering of, the process of birth, whether it be that of a child, a creative idea, or an endeavor.

Ren Mai is also known as the Sea of Yin and thus has a strong effect on the proper functioning of the Yin meridians.

In addition to providing Qi to all of your peripheral nerves (those outside your spinal column), the Conception Vessel also governs menstruation and the development of the fetus.

Imbalances in the Conception Vessel sometimes manifest as disorders of the peripheral nervous system (shingles, neuropathy), difficulties conceiving and menstruating (such problems may also be related to other meridians, including Kidney, Liver, Triple Warmer, or Pericardium), and as pain or weakness in the front and middle of the body.

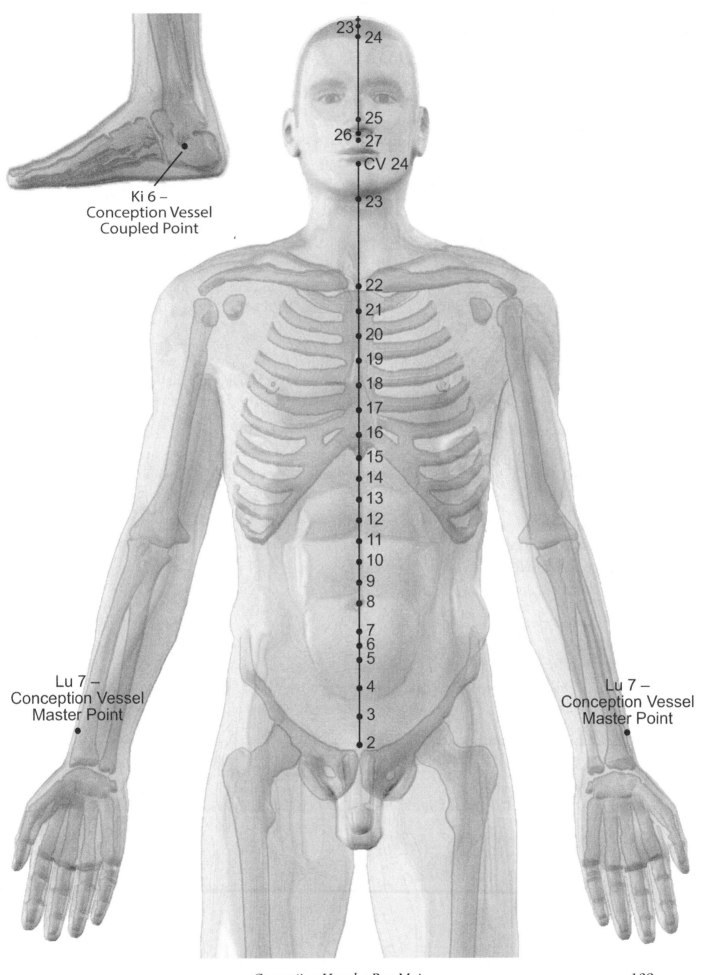

Ki 6 –
Conception Vessel
Coupled Point

Lu 7 –
Conception Vessel
Master Point

Lu 7 –
Conception Vessel
Master Point

23
24
25
26 27
CV 24
23
22
21
20
19
18
17
16
15
14
13
12
11
10
9
8
7
6
5
4
3
2

Conception Vessel - Ren Mai

Conception Vessel Point Index

All Conception Vessel points are located along the midline.

CV 1 會陰 Huiyin "Yin Meeting"

On the perineum, at the midpoint between the root of the scrotum and the anus in males, and at the midpoint between the posterior labial commissure and the anus in females.

Special Point for Breathing Stopped

Constipation, Headache, Hemorrhoids, Mucous Discharge, Period Painful or Irregular.

CV 2 曲骨 Qugu "Crooked Bone"

On the midline on the superior border of the pubic symphysis.

Breathing Stopped, Bladder Inflammation, Mucous Discharge, Semen Leakage, Uterine Hemorrhage, Uterus Remains Large After Childbirth, Womb Inflammation.

CV 3 中極 Zhongji "Middle Extremity"

3 fingers superior to CV 2.

Abdominal Inflammation, Bladder Inflammation, Edema, Female Sterility, Period Painful, Placenta Retention (Postpartum), Semen Leakage, Uterine Pain (Postpartum).

CV 4 關元 Guanyuan "Origin Pass"

3 fingers superior to CV 3.

Breathing Stopped, Colitis, Edema, Indigestion, Intestinal Hemorrhage, Kidney Inflammation, Mucous Discharge, Semen Leakage, Testicle Inflammation, Urinary Problems, Weakness.

CV 5 石門 Shimen "Stone Gate"

3 fingers superior to CV 4.

All Genitourinary Problems.

Cecum Inflamed, Enterocolitis, Vomiting Blood.

CV 6 氣海 Qihai "Sea of Qi"

2 fingers superior to CV 5.

All Intestinal Problems, All Urinary Problems.

Asthma, Bladder Inflammation, Cecum Inflammation (Chronic), Colic, Depression, Enterocolitis, Intestinal Hemorrhage, Periods Painful, Semen Leakage, Uterine Hemorrhage.

CV 7 陰交 Yinjiao "Yin Intersection"

2 fingers superior to CV 6, 3 fingers inferior to CV 8.

All Genital Problems.

Dizziness (Postpartum), Periods Painful, Semen Leakage, Scrotum Pain, Urethra Inflammation.

CV 8 神闕 Shenque "Spirit Palace"

In the center of the navel.

Abdominal Inflammation, Cerebral Hemorrhage, Diarrhea, Edema, Enterocolitis, Flatulence, Rectal Prolapse, Stroke.

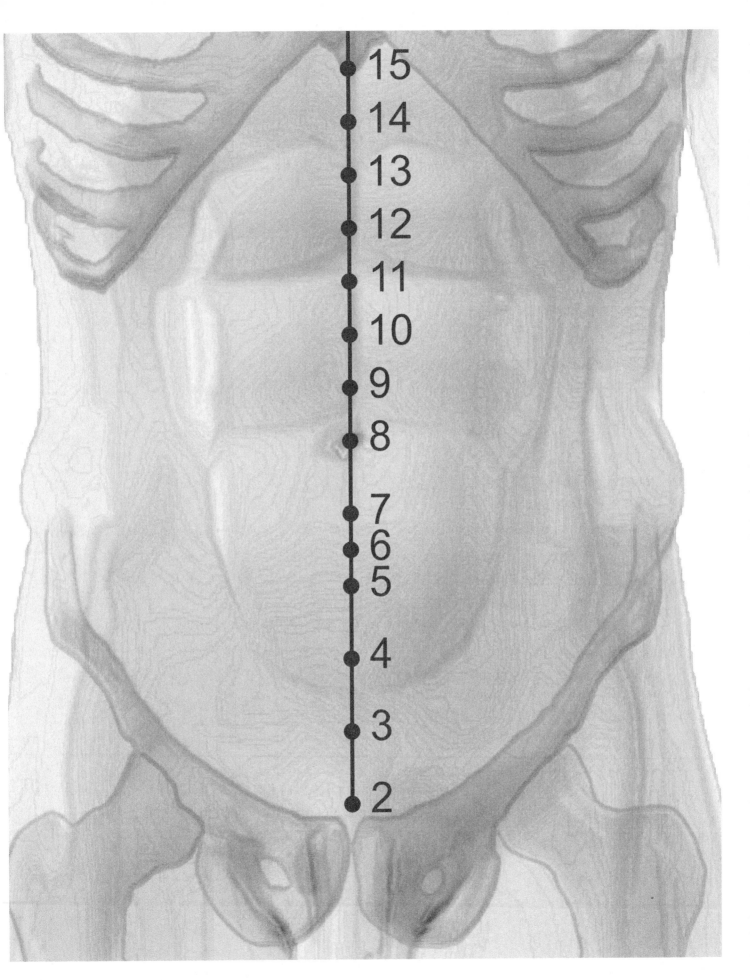

CV 9 to 14 are each 1.5 fingers or a wide finger from the previous.

CV 9 水分 Shuifen "Water Division"

2 fingers superior to CV 8

Special Point for Water Retention or Swelling (Edema).

Abdominal Inflation, Anorexia, Enterocolitis, Flatulence, Hernia, Muscle Tone Lacking, Stomach Sluggish.

CV 10 下脘 Xiawan "Lower Epigastrium"

2 fingers superior to CV 9

Enterocolitis, Indigestion, Stomach Inflammation.

CV 11 建里 Jianli "Internal Foundation"

2 fingers superior to CV 10

Edema, Indigestion, Stomach Inflammation.

CV 12 中脘 Zhongwan "Middle Epigastrium"

2 fingers superior to CV 11

All Stomach Problems, All Uterine Problems.

Anorexia, Chest Congestion (Pleurisy), Cholera, Epilepsy, Stomach Inflammation.

CV 13 上脘 Shangwan "Upper Epigastrium"

2 fingers superior to CV 12

All Stomach Problems,

Abdominal Inflammation, Bronchitis, Chest Inflammation, Enterocolitis, Epilepsy, Hernia, Kidney Inflammation.

CV 14 巨闕 Juque "Great Palace"

2 fingers superior to CV 13 or 1.5 fingers inferior to CV 15

Abdominal Inflation, Anorexia, Anxiety, Bronchitis, Diaphragm Spasm, Pericarditis, Psychopathy.

CV 15 鳩尾 Jiuwei "Bird Tail"

Just inferior to the xiphoid process (the "tail" of the sternum)—careful not to apply too much pressure to the underside of the xiphoid as this is a sensitive area.

Bronchitis, Cerebral Weakness, Epilepsy, Heart Problems, Nerve Diseases, Pulmonary Emphysema, Stomach Pain or Inflammation.

CV 16 中庭 Zhongting "Central Courtyard"

Just onto the sternum from the base of the xiphoid process, at the level of the 5th intercostal space.

Esophagus Spasm, Pulmonary Congestion, Stomach Hemorrhage, Tonsillitis, Vomiting Mother's Milk (Babies).

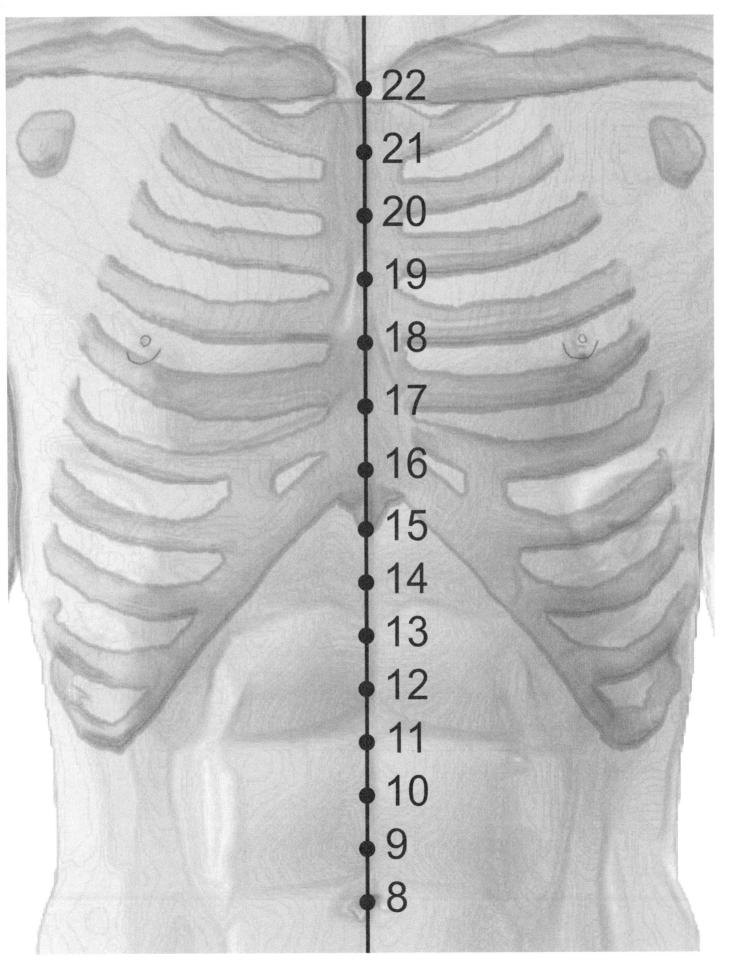

CV 17 膻中 Shanzhong "Middle of the Chest"

3 fingers superior to CV 16, 3 fingers superior to the base of the xiphoid process, at the level of the 4th intercostal space.

Anxiety, Asthma, Breast Inflammation, Bronchitis, Cough, Esophagus Spasm, Pleurisy, Pulmonary Tuberculosis, Stomach Hemorrhage, Tonsillitis, Vomiting Mother's Milk (Babies).

CV 18 玉堂 Yutang "Jade Hall"

3 fingers superior to CV 17, at the level of the 3rd intercostal space.

Bronchitis, Pleurisy, Pulmonary Congestion, Vomiting Mother's Milk.

CV 19 紫宮 Zigong "Violet Palace"

3 fingers superior to CV 18, at the level of the 2rd intercostal space.

Bronchitis, Pleurisy, Esophagus Spasm, Pulmonary Congestion, Pulmonary Tuberculosis, Stomach Hemorrhage, Tonsillitis.

CV 20 華蓋 Huagai "Splendid Cover"

3 fingers superior to CV 19, at the level of the 1st intercostal space.

Asthma, Pleurisy, Esophagus Spasm, Nasal Inflammation, Pulmonary Congestion, Smoking (To Stop).

CV 21 璇璣 Xuanji "Jade Rotator"

3 fingers superior to CV 20, just onto the sternum from the superior border.

Breathing Difficult, Chest (Sides) Painful, Cough, Pulmonary Congestion, Throat Problems, Tonsillitis.

CV 22 天突 Tiantu "Heaven Projection"

Just superior to the superior border of the sternum, pressing inferiorly and somewhat posteriorly.

All Respiratory Problems.

Asthma, Esophagus Spasm, Nasal Inflammation, Throat Problems, Tonsillitis.

CV 23 廉泉 Lianquan "Lateral Spring"

In the depression above the upper border of the hyoid bone, where the neck meets the underside of the chin.

Mouth Sores, Nasal Inflammation, Thirst Excessive, Throat Sore.

CV 24 承漿 Chengjiang "Saliva Container"

In the depression between the lower lip and the chin.

Diabetes, Epilepsy, Stroke, Toothache.

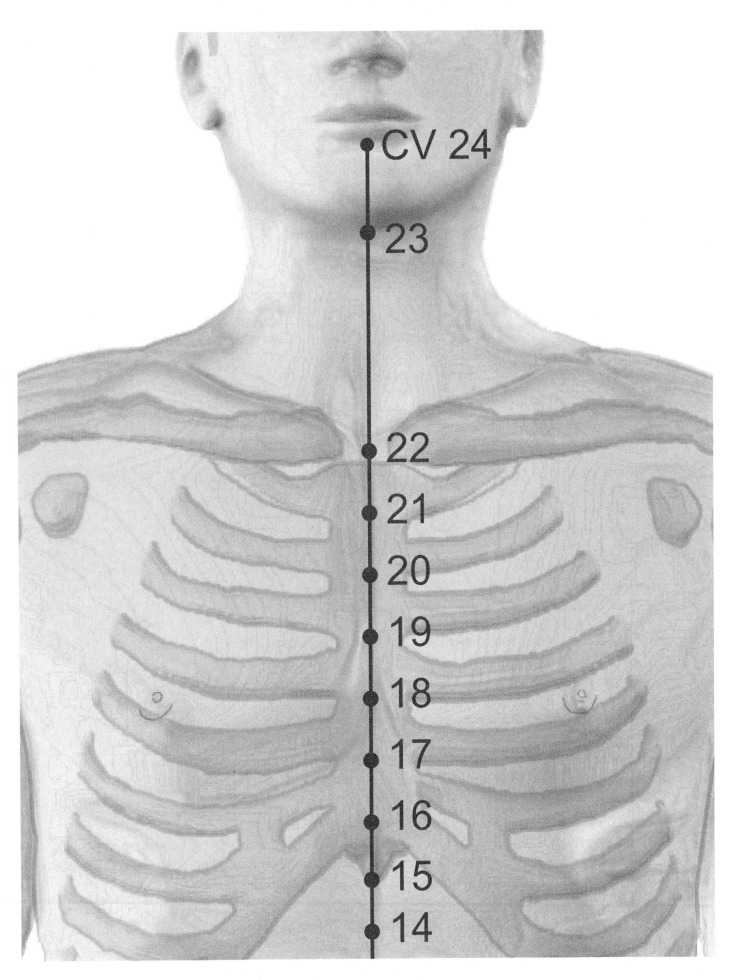

督脉
Governing Vessel (Du Mai)
Of the Great Central Channel

Master and Coupled Points

Governing Vessel Master   SI 3   Governing Vessel Coupled   Bl 62

Common Physical Symptoms of Imbalance:

Rounded Shoulders, Head Heavy (Deficiency)

Headaches and Pain In Eyes (Excess)

Stiffness in Spine (Excess)

Back Pain or Tension

Conjunctivitis

Dizziness

Eye Problems (Inner Canthus)

Extremities Cold

Fevers

Hemorrhoids

Insomnia

Neck Pain

Nervousness or Over-stimulation

Memory Poor

Spinal Problems

Common Emotional Symptoms of Imbalance:

Depression

Mania

Mortality Fears

Ungroundedness

As with the Conception Vessel, the Governing Vessel does not have a corresponding organ. In Chinese medicine, it is the regulator of the central nervous system including the brain and spinal cord and, along with the Conception Vessel and the other Extra Meridians, functions to balance the other twelve meridians by acting as an alternate path for Qi or as a pressure release like the flood plain of a river.

The Du Mai is also called the "Sea of Yang," and stores, nourishes and moves the Yang energy within the body, and influences all of the Yang Meridians. It particularly strengthens the Yang of the Kidneys, which is the root of all Yang within the body and, along with its connection with the brain, can be helpful for traumatic brain injury, memory issues, and dizziness.

Because the Governing Vessel travels along the spine, it can also prove helpful for spinal issues such as back and sacral nerve pain, sciatica, and other nerve issues related to misalignment or inflammation within the spinal column and sacroiliac joint.

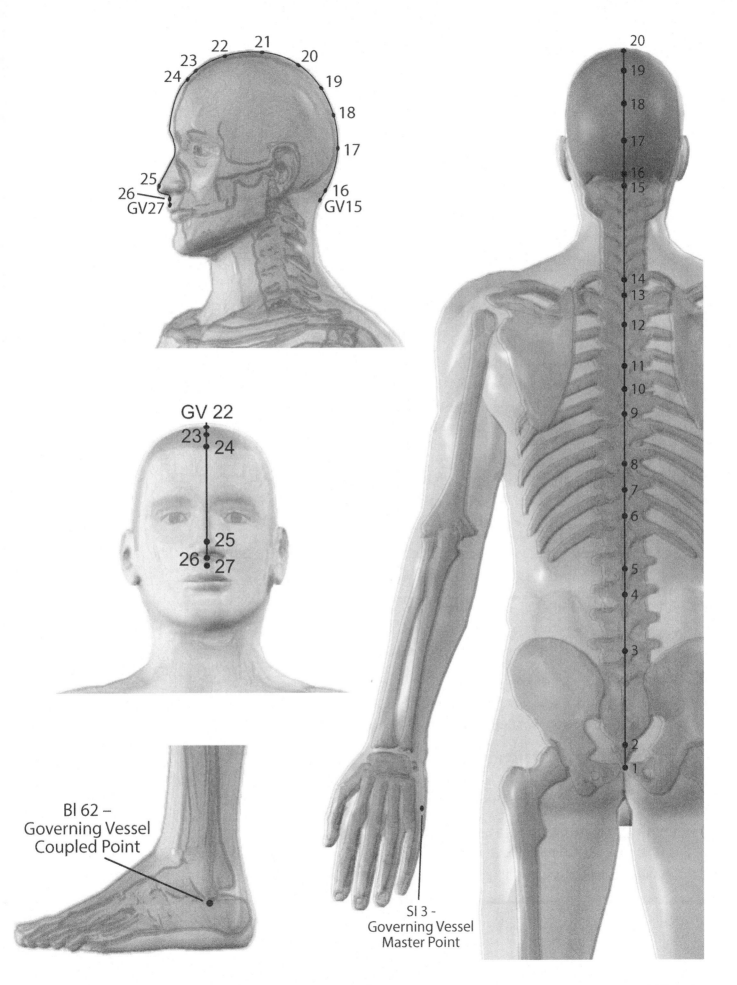

Governing Vessel - Du Mai

117

Governing Vessel Point Index

All Governing Vessel points are located along the midline.

GV 1 長強 Changqiang "Long and Rigid"

At the tip of the coccyx.

Epilepsy, Hemorrhoids, Intestinal Hemorrhage, Lower Back Pain, Semen Leakage, Vomiting.

GV 2 腰俞 Yaoshu "Low Back Transporter"

At the base of the coccyx, where the sacrum meets the coccyx.

Adrenal Exhaustion, Back Pain, Hemorrhoids, Mucous Discharge, Periods Stopped.

GV 3 腰陽關 Yaoyangquan "Low Back Yang Passage"

Between the spinous processes of L4 & L5— at the same level as Bl 25 the LI Shu point.

Abdomen Inflammation, Colitis, Enterocolitis, Lumbago.

GV 4 命門 Mingmen "Life Gate"

Between the spinous processes of L2 & 3—at the same level as Bl 23 the Ki Shu point..

Deafness, Ears Ring, Headache, Hemorrhoids, Hernia, Insomnia, Meningitis, Semen Leakage, Skin Dry, Urinary Incontinence, Vaginal Discharge.

GV 5 懸樞 Xuanshu "Suspended Pivot"

Between the spinous processes of L1 and 2—at the same level as Bl 22 the TW Shu point.

Back Pain, Colic, Diarrhea, Enterocolitis, Stomach Ache.

GV 6 脊中 Jizhong "Middle of the Spine"

Between the spinous processes of T11 & T12—at the same level as Bl 20 the Sp Shu point.

Epilepsy, Hemorrhoids, Jaundice, Rectal Prolapse.

GV 7 中樞 Zhongshu "Central Pivot"

Between the spinous processes of T10 & T11—at the same level as Bl 19 the GB Shu point.

Back Pain, Eyesight Deterioration, Stomach Ache.

GV 8 筋縮 Jinsuo "Muscle Spasm"

Between the spinous processes of T9 & T10—at the same level as Bl 18 the Lv Shu point.

Back Pain, Depression, Epilepsy, Stomach Spasm.

GV 9 至陽 Zhiyang "Reaching Yang"

Between the spinous processes of T7 & T8—at the same level as Bl 17 the Diaphragm Shu point.

Abdomen Cold, Abdomen Pain, Anorexia, Back Pain, Flatulence, Jaundice.

GV 10 靈台 Lingtai "Spirit Platform"

Between the spinous processes of T6 & T7—at the same level as Bl 16 the GV Shu point.

Asthma, Bronchitis, Cold Exposure, Pneumonia, Pulmonary Tuberculosis.

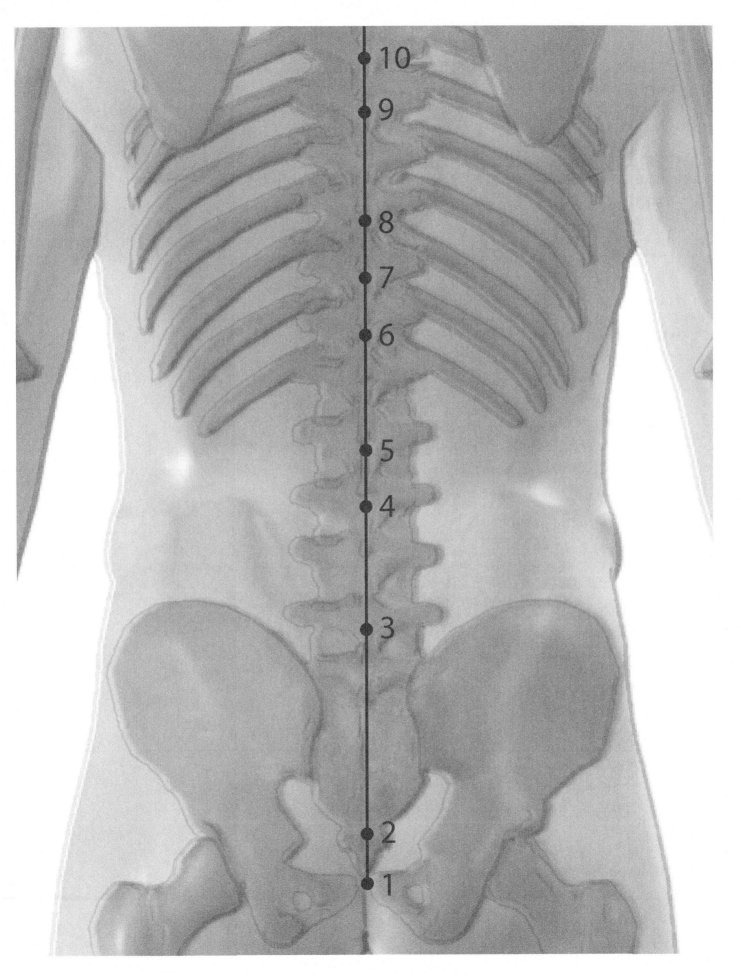

GV 11 神道 Shendao "Way of the Spirit"

Between the spinous processes of T5 & T6—at the same level as Bl 15 the Ht Shu point.

Brain Problems, Bronchitis, Cerebral Weakness, Enterocolitis, Headache, Heart Problems, Insomnia, Jaw Inflammation.

GV 12 身柱 Shenzhu "Body Pillar"

Between the spinous processes of T3 & T4—at the same level as Bl 13 the Lu Shu point.

All Brain Problems.

Cerebral Weakness, Epilepsy, Night Fever, Nosebleed.

GV 13 陶道 Taodao "Way of the Pot"

Between the spinous processes of T1 & T2.

Depression, Malaria.

GV 14 大椎 Dazhui "Great Vertebra"

Between the spinous processes of C7 & T1.

Asthma, Cold Exposure, Gums Inflamed, Jaundice, Malaria, Nosebleed, Psychopathy, Pulmonary Emphysema, Vomiting.

GV 15 瘖門 (啞門) Yamen "Mutism Gate"

At the base of the occiput.

Cerebral Congestion, Epilepsy, Headache (Chronic), Marrow Inflamed, Meningitis, Nosebleed, Pharyngitis, Stroke.

GV 16 風府 Fengfu "Wind Palace"

Inferior to the occipital protuberance (bump on back of head).

Epilepsy, Fever after Cold Exposure, Headache, Jaundice, Neck Pain, Nosebleed, Pharyngitis, Psychopathy, Stroke, Teeth Grinding, Toothache.

GV 17 腦戶 Naohu "Brain Door"

4 fingers superior to GV 16.

Eye Problems, Headache, Neck Stiff & Pain, Psychopathy.

GV 18 強間 Qiangjian "Rigid Space"

4 fingers superior to GV 17.

Depression, Dizziness, Epilepsy (Children), Headache, Vomiting.

GV 19 後頂 Houding "Back Vertex"

4 fingers superior to GV 18.

Cerebral Congestion, Dizziness, Epilepsy, Migraine.

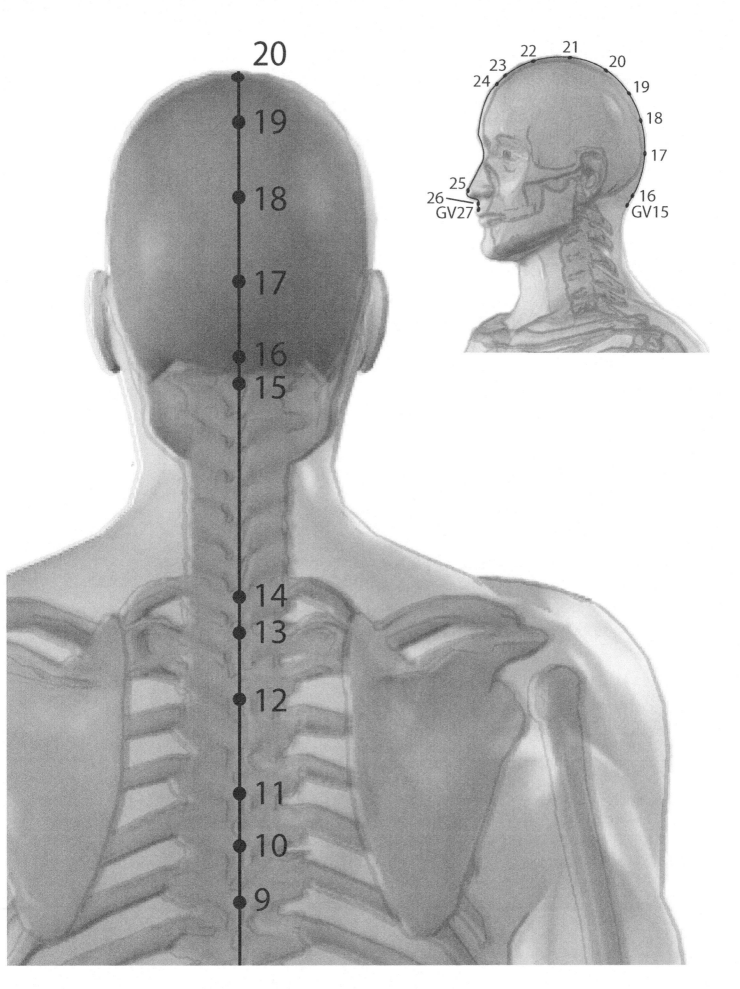

Governing Vessel - Du Mai

GV 20 百會 Baihui "One Hundred Meetings"

4 fingers superior to GV 17, on the top of the head.

Cerebral Anemia, Dizziness, Epilepsy, Headache, Hemorrhoids, Memory Poor, Rectal Prolapse, Stroke, Uterine Prolapse.

GV 21 前頂 Qianding "Front Vertex"

4 fingers anterior to GV 20.

Cerebral Anemia or Congestion, Dizziness, Headache, Nasal Polyps, Nervousness in Children.

GV 22 囟會 Xinhui "Fontanelle Meeting"

4 fingers anterior to GV 21.

Anemic Headache, Dizziness, Epilepsy, Nervousness, Nosebleed, Sleep Excessive.

GV 23 上星 Shangxing "Upper Star"

3 fingers anterior to GV 22, 2 fingers posterior to the hairline.

Dizziness, Eye Congestion, Fever, Film over Eye, Headache, Nasal Polyps, Nosebleed.

GV 24 神庭 Shenting "Spirit Courtyard"

2 fingers anterior to GV 23, at the hairline.

Anxiety, Eye Problems, Epilepsy, Headache, Insomnia, Nasal Inflammation, Tear Glands Inflamed.

GV 25 素髎 Suliao "Plain Space"

The tip of the nose.

Boil on Nose, Nasal Polyps, Nasal Sores, Nosebleeds, Nose Stuffy, Tears Excessive or Deficient, Vomiting.

GV 26 人中 Renzhong "Middle of the Person"

Just inferior to the nose (⅓ distance inferiorly of the philtrum).

Revival Point.

Cerebral Congestion, Diabetes, Edema, Epilepsy, Eye Muscle Problems, Hysteria, Spinal Pain, Stroke, Toothache.

GV 27 兌端 Duiduan "End Exchange"

At the juncture of the upper lip and the philtrum.

Revival/Shock Point.

Delirium, Epilepsy, Fainting, Hysteria, Jaundice, Mouth Sores, Nosebleeds, Shock, Thirst Excessive, Tongue Dry, Toothache.

GV 28 齦交 Yinjiao "Gum Union"

Directly behind GV 27 on the upper gum. Pressing on GV 72 also presses on GV 28

Revival Point; Eyes Itch, Eye Problems, Film over Eye, Nasal Polyps, Neck Pain, Nose Stuffy, Tears Excessive or Deficient.

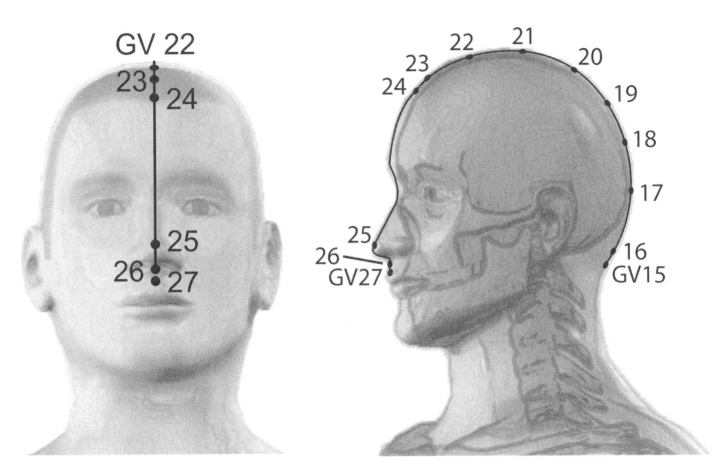

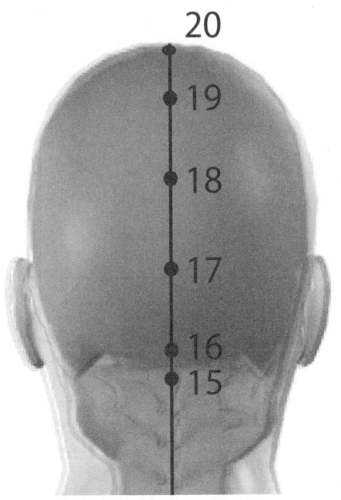

Governing Vessel - Du Mai

维脉
Wei Mai (Linking Vessel)

Master and Coupled Points

Yin Wei Mai Master	Pc 6	Yang Wei Mai Master	TW 5
Yin Wei Mai Coupled	Sp 4	Yang Wei Mai Coupled	GB 41

Common Symptoms of Imbalance:

Yin Wei Mai
Anxiety or Apprehension
Cardiac Pain
Digestive Problems
Emotional Instability
Nervousness or Timidity
Varicose Veins
Genital Pain (Deficient)

Yang Wei Mai
Acne
Boils
Chills & Fever
Earache
Frequent/Severe Illness
Lymphatic Problems
Neck Tension
Thinness
Weakness
Coldness, Chills, Colds (Deficient)
Low Resistance (Deficient)

Common Emotional Symptoms of Imbalance:

Yin Wei Mai
Anxiety
Depression
Emotional Instability
Insomnia
Nervousness or Timidity
Poor Memory

Yang Wei Mai
Anger
Bipolar Disorder
Indecision
Passive-Aggressive Behavior

The Yin and Yang Wei Mai function as connecting vessels for and between the body's interior (Yin) and exterior (Yang) Qi.

The Yin Linking Vessel nourishes the Blood and the Yin that circulates; Because of the Heart-Blood connection, mental stress, including anxiety, insomnia and depression, is cleared through this vessel.

The Yang Linking Vessel governs the exterior of the body and supports the immune system in fending off and dispelling illnesses (Wei Qi is translated as Defensive Qi).

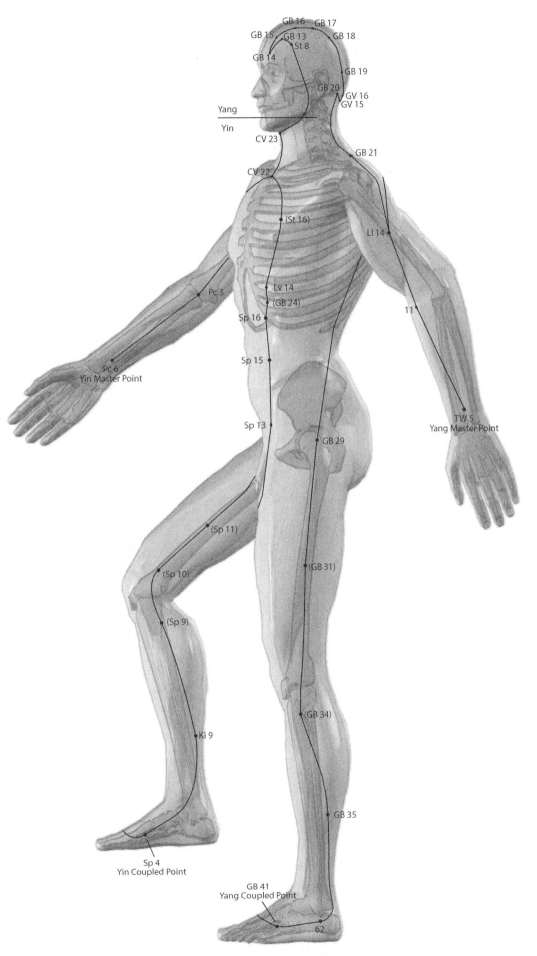

GB 16
GB 17
GB 15
GB 13
GB 18
GB 14
St 8
GB 19
GB 20
GV 16
Yang
GV 15
Yin
CV 23
GB 21
CV 22
LI 14
(St 16)
Lv 14
Pc 3
(GB 24)
11
Sp 16
Sp 15
Sp 13
GB 29
TW 5
Yang Master Point
Pc 6
Yin Master Point
(Sp 11)
(GB 31)
(Sp 10)
(Sp 9)
(GB 34)
Ki 9
GB 35
Sp 4
Yin Coupled Point
GB 41
Yang Coupled Point
62

Wei Mai - Linking Vessel

125

Yin Wei Mai Point Index

Master Point:

Pc 6 內關 Neiguan "Inner Pass"

3 fingers proximally from the center of the crease of the wrist.

Emotional Problems, Menstrual Irregularity, Psychological Problems, Elbow pain, Endocarditis, Eye Hemorrhage, Hiccups, Jaundice, Myocarditis, Stomach Pain.

Coupled Point:

Sp 4 公孫 Gongsun "Grandfather Grandson" (Lo Point)

Trace along the underside of the shaft of the first metatarsal toward the heel to where the shaft meets the proximal head. Pressing into shaft, head and inferiorly into the tissue.

Abdominal Swelling, Anorexia, Edema (Head), Epilepsy, Heart Inflammation, Hemorrhoids, Intestinal Hemorrhage, Pleurisy (Chest Inflammation), Stomach Cancer, Vomiting.

Points:

Points in parentheses indicate they are not traditional points but are considered points on the vessel by some experts. They seem effective when releasing the vessel.

Ki 9 築賓 Zhubin "Strong Knees"

8 fingers superior to the crown of the medial malleolus and 4 fingers posterior to the tibia in the lower gastrocnemius.

Dementia, Chronic Conditions, Poisoning, Psychopathy.

(Sp 9 陰陵泉 Yinlingquan "Yin Mound Spring")

On the posterior edge of the tibia, in the angle where the shaft meets the head.

Abdomen Cold, Cramp, Insomnia, Legs Weak, Urinary Suppression, Vaginitis.

(Sp 10 血海 Xuehai "Sea of Blood")

From the superior medial corner of the patella, 3 fingers medial and 3 fingers inferior.

Abdomen Pain, Period Painful, Pleurisy, Testicle Inflammation, Womb Inflammation.

(Sp 11 箕門 Jimen "Separation Gate")

7 fingers superior to Sp 10.

Bladder Problems, Mucous Discharge, Swollen Glands (Groin).

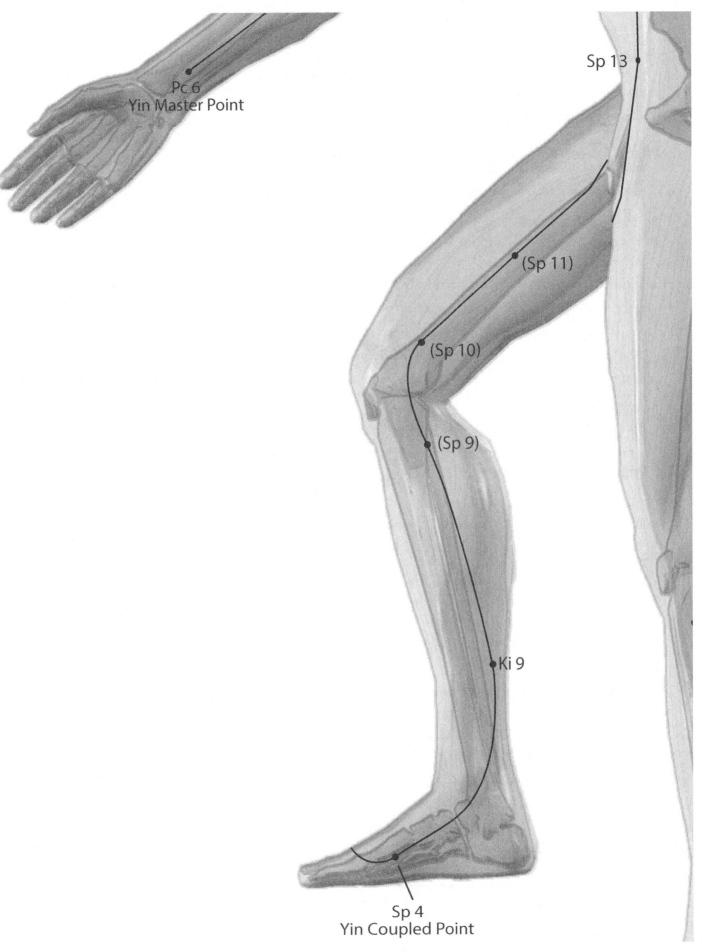

Pc 6
Yin Master Point

Sp 13

(Sp 11)

(Sp 10)

(Sp 9)

Ki 9

Sp 4
Yin Coupled Point

Sp 13 府舍 Fushe "Bowel Abode"

Just superior to the inguinal ligament, 4 fingers laterally and 3 fingers superiorly from the lateral corner of the pubic bone.

Cecum Inflammation, Cholera, Constipation, Spleen Inflammation.

Sp 15 大橫 Da heng "Great Horizontal"

6 fingers lateral to the umbilicus.

Constipation, Diarrhea (Chronic), Enterocolitis (Acute), Influenza, Sweat Excessive.

Sp 16 腹哀 Fuai "Abdomen Suffering"

5 fingers lateral to the midline at the height where you touch the edge of the rib cage, in the niche between the attachment of the 9th and 10th ribs.

Blood in Stools, Intestinal Hemorrhage, Stomach Hyperacid, Ulcer.

(GB 24 日月 Riyue "Sun and Moon")

On the mammillary line (line running vertically through the nipple), between the 7th and 8th ribs (the lowest intercostal space on that line) 8 fingers laterally from the midline.

Depression, Hernia, Jaundice, Liver Problems, Stomach & Abdomen Problems.

Lv 14 期門 Qimen "Cyclic Gate"

In the 6th intercostal space (between 6th and 7th ribs) on the mammillary line.

Abdominal Inflammation, Breathing Difficult, Chest Inflammation, Cough, Hypertension, Kidney Inflammation, Vomiting after Meals.

(St 16 膺窗 Yingchuang "Breast Window")

In the 3nd intercostal space on St 11 on the mammillary line.

Breast Tumor, Emphysema, Flatulence, Pulmonary Congestion.

CV 22 天突 Tiantu "Heaven Projection"

On the midline, just superior to the superior border of the sternum, pressing inferiorly and somewhat posteriorly.

All Respiratory Problems, Asthma, Esophagus Spasm, Nasal Inflammation, Throat Problems, Tonsillitis.

CV 23 廉泉 Lianquan "Lateral Spring"

On the midline, in the depression above the upper border of the hyoid bone, where the neck meets the underside of the chin.

Mouth Sores, Nasal Inflammation, Thirst Excessive, Throat Sore.

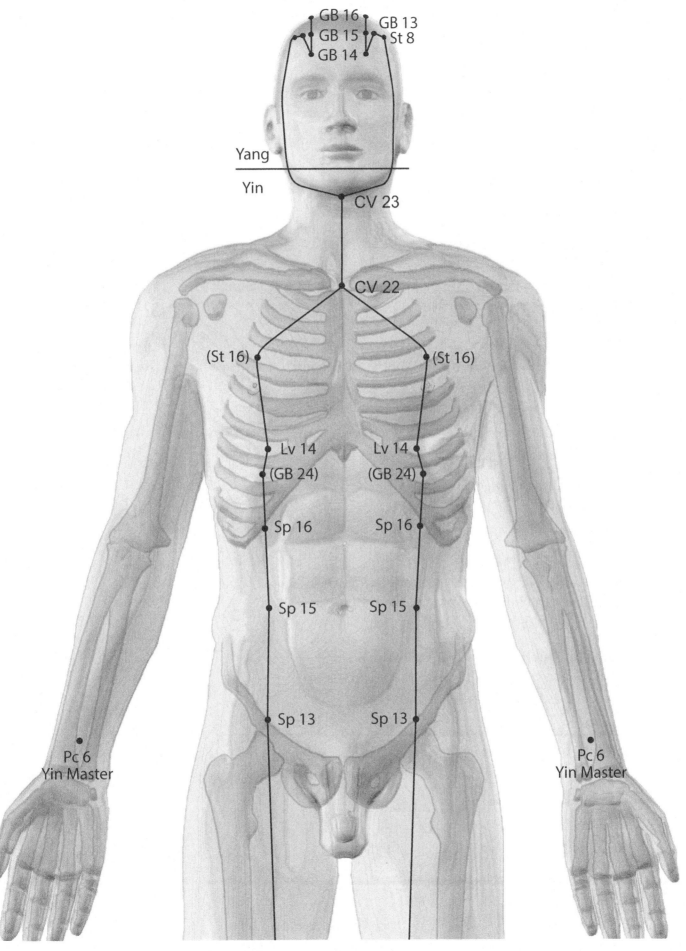

GB 16
GB 13
GB 15
St 8
GB 14

Yang

Yin

CV 23

CV 22

(St 16)
(St 16)

Lv 14
Lv 14
(GB 24)
(GB 24)

Sp 16
Sp 16

Sp 15
Sp 15

Sp 13
Sp 13

Pc 6
Yin Master

Pc 6
Yin Master

Wei Mai - Linking Vessel

Yang Wei Mai Point Index

Master Point:

TW 5 外關 Waiguan "Outer Pass"

5 fingers proximal from the center of the crease of the wrist and TW 4, between the radius and the ulna.

Arthritis (Arm), Deafness, Eye Problems, Toothache

Coupled Point:

GB 41 足臨泣 Zulinqi "Foot Governor of Tears"

On the top of the foot, the most proximal end of the space between the 4th and 5th metatarsals.

All Skin Diseases, Pain, Breathing Problems, Breast Inflammation, Dizziness, Endocarditis, Fever, Headache, Periods Painful, Scrofula.

Points:

Points in parentheses indicate they are not traditional points but are considered points on the vessel by some experts. They seem effective when releasing the vessel.

St 8 頭維 Touwei "Head's Corner"

On the hairline corner, 4 fingers laterally from the corner of the eye and superiorly 6 fingers.

Cerebral Congestion, Conjunctivitis, Migraine, Vision Problems.

GB 13 本神 Benshen "Root of the Spirit"

2 fingers lateral from GB 15 at the hairline.

Epilepsy, Dizziness, Headache.

GB 14 陽白 Yangbai "Yang White"

Starting at the eyebrow above the center of the eye, locate the point In the depression of the forehead 1/2 way from the eyebrow to the hairline,.

Eye Problems, Facial Spasm, Headache.

GB 15 頭臨泣 Toulinqi "Head Governor of Tears"

Located 3 fingers superior to GB 14 at the hairline.

Epilepsy, Eyes Water Excessively, Stroke.

GB 16 目窗 Muchuang "Window of the Eye"

Located 4 fingers posterior to GB 15.

Abscess, Dizziness, Eyesight Weak, Fever (From Cold Exposure), Headache.

GB 17 正營 Zhengying "Upright Nutrition"

Located 3 fingers posterior to GB 16.

Dizziness, Eyesight Weak, Headache, Toothache.

GB 18 承靈 Chengling "Support Spirit"

Located 4 fingers posterior to GB 17.

Breathing Difficult, Coldness, Fever, Headache, Nosebleed.

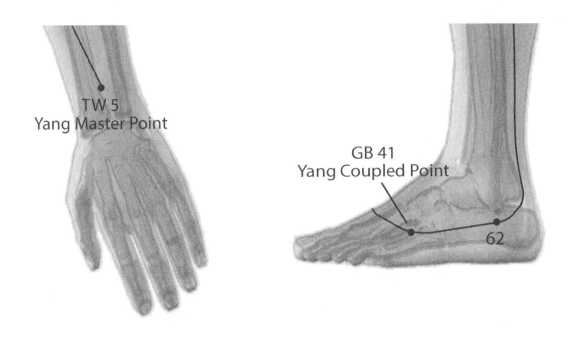

TW 5
Yang Master Point

GB 41
Yang Coupled Point

62

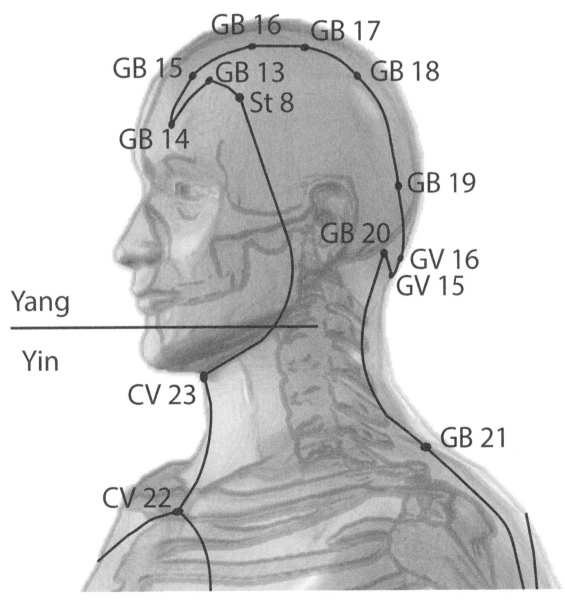

GB 16   GB 17

GB 15   GB 13   GB 18
         St 8

GB 14

GB 19

GB 20
         GV 16
         GV 15

Yang

Yin

CV 23

GB 21

CV 22

GB 19 腦空 Naokong "Brain Hollow"

Located 4 fingers superior to GB 20.

Anxiety, Breathing Difficult, Coldness, Fever, Headache, Nosebleed.

GV 16 風府 Fengfu "Wind Palace"

Inferior to the occipital protuberance (bump on back of head) on the midline.

Epilepsy, Fever after Cold Exposure, Headache, Jaundice, Neck Pain, Nosebleed, Pharyngitis, Psychopathy, Stroke, Teeth Grinding, Toothache.

GV 15 瘂門 (啞門) Yamen "Mutism Gate"

At the base of the occiput on the midline.

Cerebral Congestion, Epilepsy, Headache (Chronic), Marrow Inflamed, Meningitis, Nosebleed, Pharyngitis, Stroke.

GB 20 風池 Fengchi "Wind Pool"

Located on the lateral edge of the attachment of the trapezius to the occiput, or 4 fingers from the midline, at the base of the skull.

Special Point for All Brain Disorders.
Ear, Eye or Nose Problems, Ears Ring, Headache, Stroke.

GB 21 肩井 Jianjing "Shoulder Well"

Located at the most superior aspect of the shoulder, finger from the base of the neck.

Brain Weakness, Breast Inflammation, Neck & Shoulder Muscle Problems, Uterine Hemorrhage.

LI 14 臂臑 Binao "Upper Arm"

From the lateral middle area of the upper arm, grasp the inner and outer sides of the deltoid muscle and follow them distally to where they come together and attach to the humerus, forming the bottom of a V. LI 14 is 2 fingers to the anterior of the attachment point of the V pressing into the humerus.

Arm Neuralgia, Arthritis, Headache, Scrofula, Sore Throat.

LI 11 曲池 Quchi "Pool at the Bend" - Tonification point, Earth point

Hold your arm as if it were in a sling, then follow across on the superior line of the forearm (along the radius) proximally toward the elbow until you reach the elbow (humerus) just anterior to the biceps tendon. The point is located distally 3 fingers and pressing into the radius bone

Anemia, Pressure on Brain, Chest Infection, Constipation, Depression, Headache, Intercostal Neuralgia, Lateral Paralysis, Scapula Pain, Shoulder Pain, Skin Problems, Tonsillitis, Toothache.

GB 29 居髎 Juliao "Stationary Crevice"

Just superior to the greater trochanter of the femur (where you feel the hip bone on the side of the hip).

Bladder Inflammation, Cecum Inflammation, Kidney Inflammation, Periods Painful, Testicle Inflammation, Uterine Problems, Vaginal Discharge.

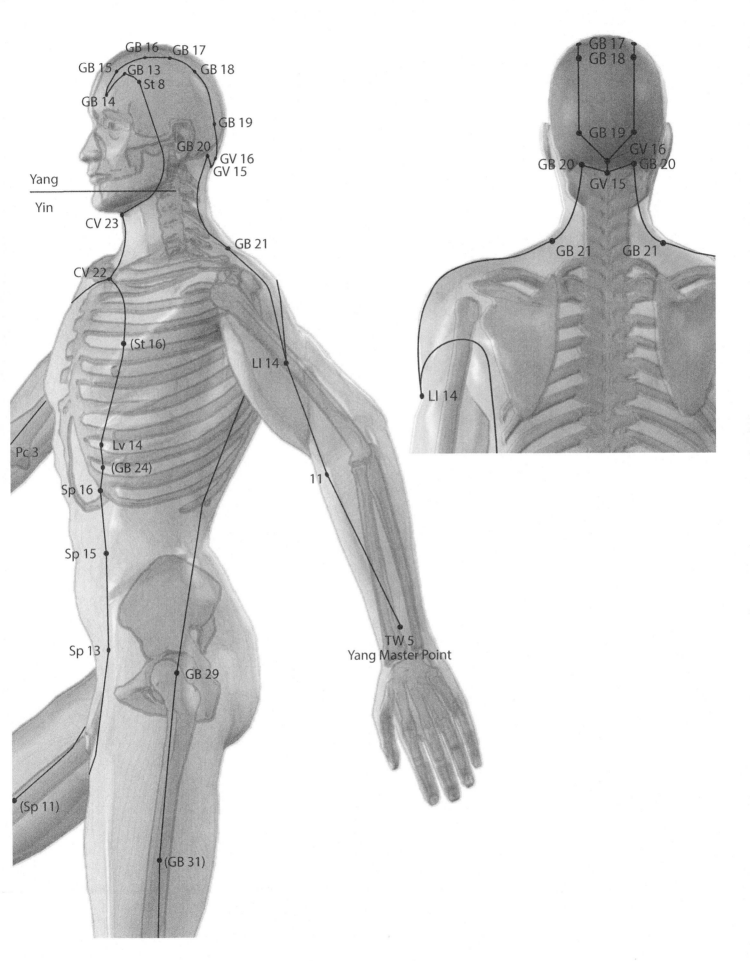

Wei Mai - Linking Vessel

133

(GB 31 風市 Fengshi "Wind Market")

Standing with your arms at your sides, where the proximal joint of the middle finger touches the leg. Feel around for the sore spot.

Leg Spasm.

(GB 34 陽陵泉 Yanglingquan "Yang Mound Spring")

Just anterior to the bump on the side of the head of the fibula, just inferior to where the fibula and tibia meet.

General Tonic, Vitality, Resistance to Disease; Special Point for Muscle Spasms; Arteriosclerosis, Chronic Constipation.

GB 35 陽交 Yangjiao "Yang Intersection"

10 fingers superiorly from the crown of the lateral malleolus, on the posterior edge of the fibula.

Breathing Difficult, Chest Inflammation, Legs Weak.

Bl 62 申脈 Shenmai "Extending Vessel"

Directly inferior to the lateral malleolus.

Stroke.

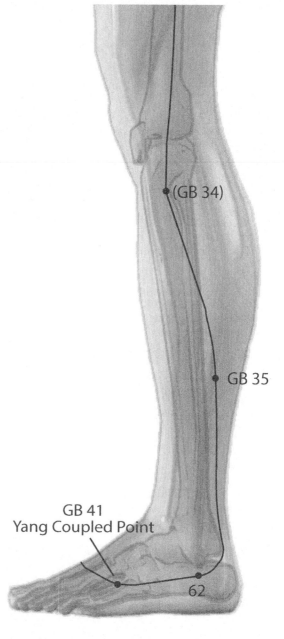

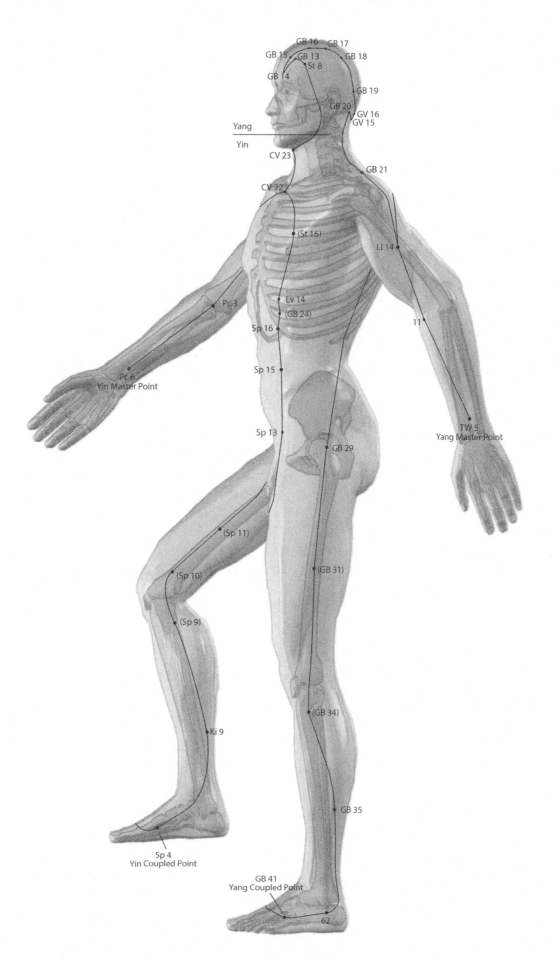

Wei Mai - Linking Vessel

跷脉
Qiao Mai (Heel Vessel)

Master and Coupled Points

Yin Qiao Mai Master	Ki 6	Yang Qiao Mai Master	Bl 62
Yin Qiao Mai Coupled	Bl 62	Yang Qiao Mai Coupled	Ki 6

Common Symptoms of Imbalance:

Yin Qiao Mai
Constipation
Fatigue, Sleepiness Excessive
Kidney Problems
Menstrual Problems
Prostate Problems
Pregnancy & Postpartum Problems
Sexual Problems (Impotence, Lack of
Desire, Genital Disorders)
Lack of Vitality (Deficiency)

Yang Qiao Mai
Cramps, Stiffness
Eyes Sore
Hormonal Imbalance
Insomnia
Joint Pain
Paranoia
Rheumatism & Arthritis
Sciatica
Testicle or Ovary Problems
Insomnia or Hyperactivity (Deficiency)

Common Emotional Symptoms of Imbalance:

Yin Qiao Mai
Self-trust Issues
Fear of Abandonment
Depression
Feelings of Unworthiness

Yang Qiao Mai
Excessive Thinking, Obsessions
Feeling Overwhelmed
Feeling Out Of Control
Mood Swings (Extreme), Bipolar

The Yin and Yang Qiao Mai function as connecting vessels between the upper and lower parts of the body, balancing excess and deficiency in either as well as between them. One indication of their interconnection is that each uses the Master point of the other as their Coupled point.

The Yin Heel Vessel absorbs excess Qi from the abdomen, hence its relationship to the reproductive organs, Kidney and Large Intestine.

The Yang Heel Vessel absorbs excess Yang Qi from the head, hence its relationship to emotional issues and insomia.

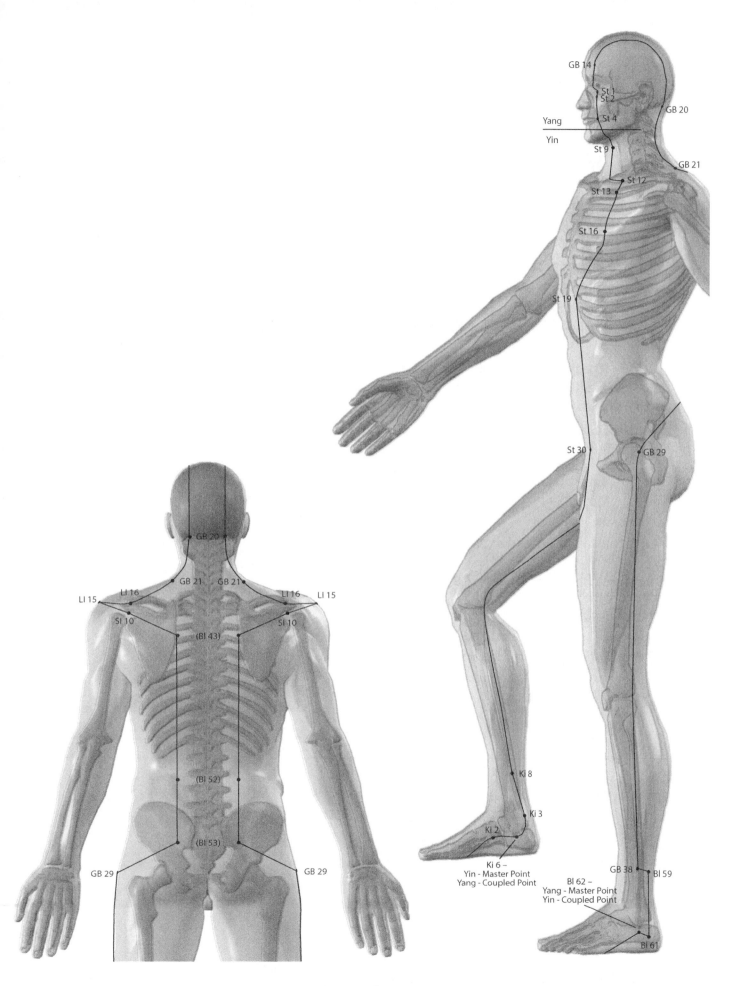

Qiao Mai - Heel Vessel

Yin Qiao Mai Point Index

Master Point:

Ki 6 照海 Zhaohai "Shining Sea"

Just inferior to the medial malleolus.

Epilepsy, Erection Involuntary, Fatigue in Limbs, Hernia, Insomnia, Mucous Discharge, Painful Period, Psychopathy, Tonsillitis, Throat Dry.

Coupled Point:

Bl 62 申脈 Shenmai "Extending Vessel"

Directly inferior to the lateral malleolus.

Stroke.

Points:

Ki 2 然谷 Rangu "Blazing Valley"

In the medial arch, in the belly of the abductor hallucis just inferior to the niche where the 1st cuneiform and the navicular bones meet.

Bladder Infection, Convulsions (Children), Diabetes, Heart Inflammation, Periods Painful, Pharyngitis, Sperm Insufficient, Testes Inflamed, Uterine Congestion, Tonsillitis, Vaginal Itch.

Ki 3 太谿 Taixi "Great Stream"

In the groove halfway between the peak of the medial malleolus and the Achilles tendon. You'll feel a little bead there.

Anorexia, Breathing Difficult, Cold Extremities, Constipation, Cough, Endocarditis, Insomnia.

Ki 8 交信 Jiaoxin "Intersecting with Spleen"

From Sp 6 (6 fingers above the peak of the medial malleolus on the edge of the tibia), 2 fingers posterior and 2 fingers inferior.

Constipation, Intestinal Inflammation, Marrow inflamed, Menstruation Excessive, Mucous Discharge, Periods Painful, Urinary Blockage.

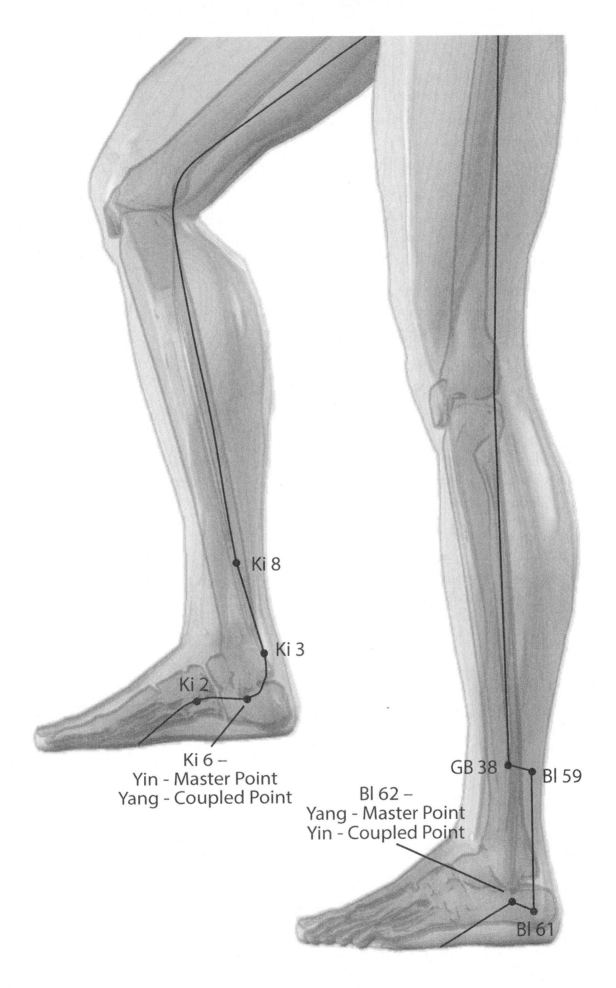

Ki 8

Ki 3

Ki 2

Ki 6 –
Yin - Master Point
Yang - Coupled Point

GB 38

Bl 59

Bl 62 –
Yang - Master Point
Yin - Coupled Point

Bl 61

Qiao Mai - Heel Vessel

St 30 氣沖 Qichong "Qi Surge"

Just superior to the outside corner of the pubic bone.

Abdominal Pain, All Genital Problems, Hernia, Impotency, Lumbago.

All Respiratory Problems.

Asthma, Esophagus Spasm, Nasal Inflammation, Throat Problems, Tonsillitis.

St 19 不容 Burong "Not Contained"

5 fingers diagonally inferior and medial to St 18. Measure 4 fingers laterally from the midline to the level where you are on the edge of the rib cage.

Anorexia, Breathing Difficult, Cough, Vomiting.

St 16 膺窗 Yingchuang "Breast Window"

3 fingers to the nipple, between the 3rd and 4th ribs - 3nd intercostal space.

Breast Tumor, Emphysema, Flatulence, Pulmonary Congestion.

St 13 氣戶 Qihu "Door of Breath"

On the inferior aspect of the clavicle directly inferior to St 12.

Resuscitation, Bronchitis, Cough, Diaphragm Spasm, Hiccups, Pulmonary Congestion.

St 12 缺盆 Quepen "Empty Basin"

4 fingers laterally from the medial head of the clavicle, then just superior to the clavicle pressing posteriorly and slightly inferiorly.

Breathing Problems, Pleurisy, Scrofula.

St 9 人迎 Renying "Man'sPrognosis" (Carotid Artery)

At the pulse point on the neck, where the neck, esophagus and underside of chin meet.

Asthma, Breathing Problems, Bronchitis, Chest Fullness, Cough, Hypertension, Neck & Throat Problems, Thyroid, Tonsils, Voice Problems, Vomiting.

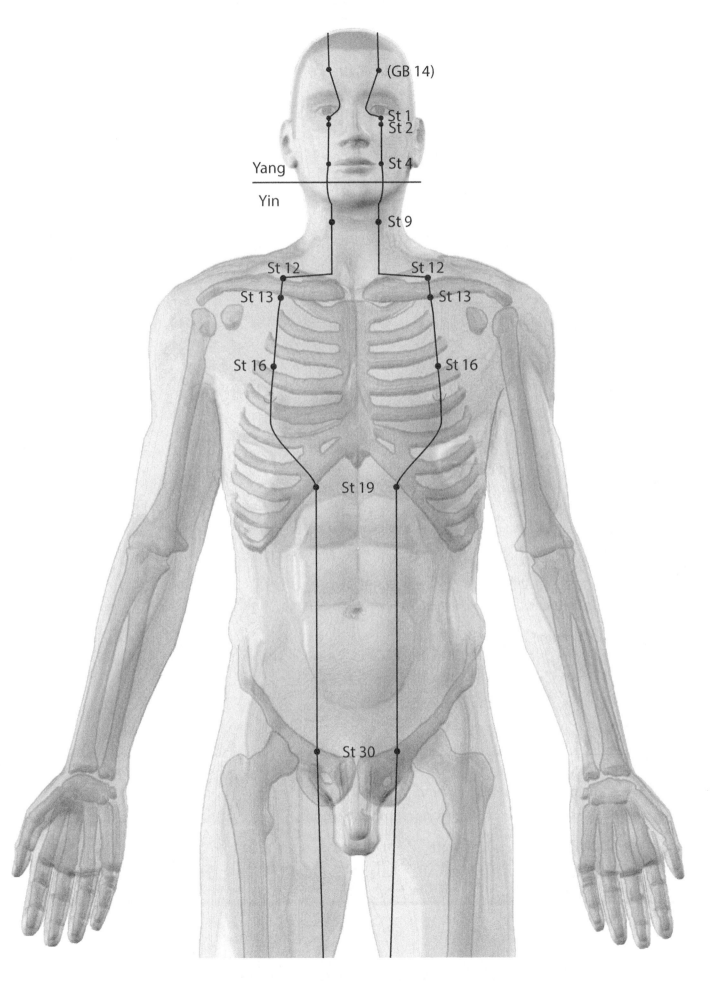

(GB 14)

St 1
St 2

St 4

Yang

Yin

St 9

St 12

St 12

St 13

St 13

St 16

St 16

St 19

St 30

Yang Qiao Mai Point Index

Master Point:

Bl 62 申脈 Shenmai "Extending Vessel"
Directly inferior to the lateral malleolus.
Stroke.

Coupled Point:

Ki 6 照海 Zhaohai "Shining Sea"
Just inferior to the medial malleolus.

Epilepsy, Erection Involuntary, Fatigue in Limbs, Hernia, Insomnia, Mucous Discharge, Painful Period, Psychopathy, Tonsillitis, Throat Dry.

Points:

Points in parentheses indicate they are not traditional points but are considered points on the vessel by some experts. They seem effective when releasing the vessel.

St 4 地倉 Dicang "Earth Granary"
At the lateral corner of the lips.
Eye Muscle Problems, Muteness, Myopia.

St 2 四白 Sibai "Four Directions Brightness"
2 fingers inferior to St 1.
Facial Abscess, Dizzy, Headache, Eye Problems, Nasal Mucous.

St 1 承泣 Chengqi "Tears Container"
Directly below the pupil on the flat of the bone.
Cornea Inflammation, Eyelid Spasm, Excessive Tears, Night Blindness.

GB 14 陽白 Yangbai "Yang White"
Starting at the eyebrow superior to the center of the eye, locate the point In the depression of the forehead 1/2 way from the eyebrow to the hairline,.
Eye Problems, Facial Spasm, Headache.

GB 20 風池 Fengchi "Wind Pool"
Located on the lateral edge of the attachment of the trapezius to the occiput, or 4 fingers lateral to the midline, at the base of the skull.
Special Point for All Brain Disorders.
Ear, Eye or Nose Problems, Ears Ring, Headache, Stroke.

GB 21 肩井 Jianjing "Shoulder Well"
Located at the most superior aspect of the shoulder, 1 finger from the base of the neck.
Brain Weakness, Breast Inflammation, Neck & Shoulder Muscle Problems, Uterine Hemorrhage.

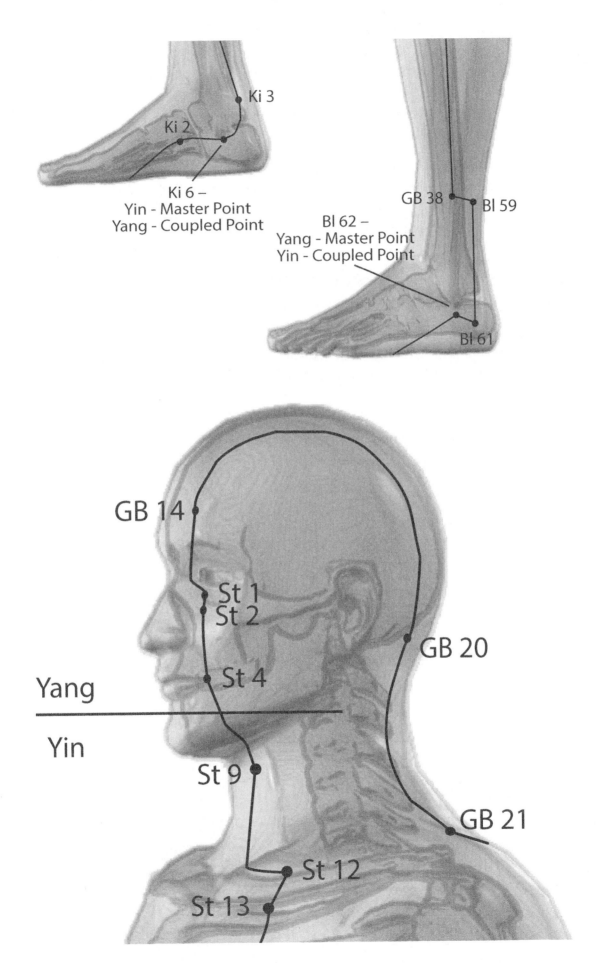

Ki 3

Ki 2

Ki 6 –
Yin - Master Point
Yang - Coupled Point

GB 38   Bl 59

Bl 62 –
Yang - Master Point
Yin - Coupled Point

Bl 61

GB 14

St 1
St 2

GB 20

St 4

Yang

Yin

St 9

GB 21

St 12

St 13

Qiao Mai - Heel Vessel

GB 29 居髎 Juliao "Stationary Crevice"

Just superior to the greater trochanter of the femur (where you feel the hip bone on the side of the hip).

Bladder Inflammation, Cecum Inflammation, Kidney Inflammation, Periods Painful, Testicle Inflammation, Uterine Problems, Vaginal Discharge.

GB 38 陽輔 Yangfu "Yang Assistance"

Measure 7 fingers superiorly from the crown (most lateral aspect) of the lateral malleolus on the anterior edge of the fibula.

Lymph Swollen (Neck), Scrofula, Tonsillitis.

Bl 59 跗陽 Fuyang "Tarsus Yang"

2 fingers inferior and 2 fingers posterior to GB 38.

Chronic Conditions.

Bl 61 僕參 Pucan "Subservient Visitor"

Halfway between the peak of the lateral malleolus and the corner of the heel in a slight depression, or 2 fingers inferior and 2 fingers posterior to Bl 62.

Knee Arthritis, Epilepsy, Shock.

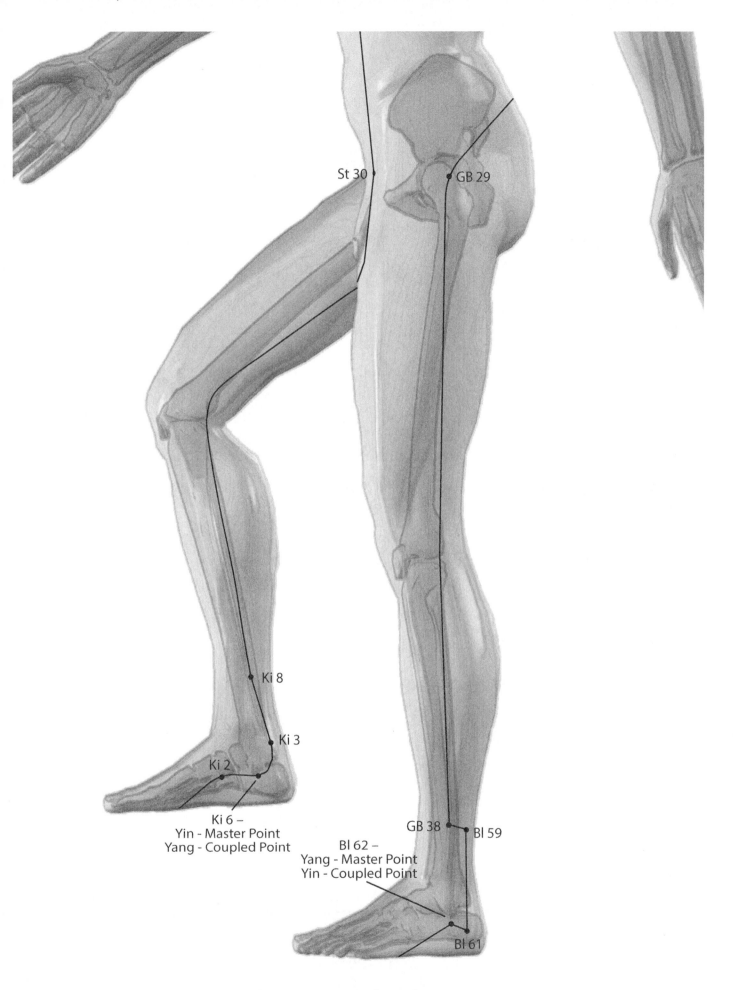

St 30

GB 29

Ki 8

Ki 3

Ki 2

Ki 6 –
Yin - Master Point
Yang - Coupled Point

GB 38

Bl 59

Bl 62 –
Yang - Master Point
Yin - Coupled Point

Bl 61

Qiao Mai - Heel Vessel

冲脉
Penetrating Vessel (Chong Mai)
带脉
Belt Vessel (Dai Mai)

Master and Coupled Points

Penetrating Master	Sp 4	Belt Master	GB 41
Penetrating Coupled	Pc 6	Belt Coupled	TW 5

Common Symptoms of Imbalance:

Penetrating Vessel	**Belt Vessel**
Appetite Loss	Abdominal Problems
Digestive Problems	Appetite Loss
Extremities Cold	Fatigue
Heart Disease	Leg & Foot Problems
Hereditary Disorders	Menstrual Problems
Gynecological Disorders	Thinness
Lumbago	Trembling
Reproductive Problems	Waist Sore
Stomach Ache	

Common Emotional Symptoms of Imbalance:

Yin Qiao Mai	**Yang Qiao Mai**
Self-trust Issues	Excessive Thinking, Obsessions
Fear of Abandonment	Feeling Overwhelmed
Depression	Feeling Out Of Control
Feelings of Unworthiness	Mood Swings (Extreme), Bipolar

The Penetrating and Belt Vessels have Ki 11 and St 30 as common points, thus affect each other.

The Penetrating Vessel is known as the "Sea of Blood" and acts as a reservoir for the Blood. Because of this, and because it originates in the uterus in women, it is indicated for any kind of gynecological disorders. Along with the Kidney meridian, it is associated with Yuan Qi, or prenatal Qi .

The Belt Vessel, also known as the Girdle Vessel, is the only horizontal vessel of the body. As such, it encircles and influences all the meridians passing through the waist and helps balance the Qi of the upper and lower body. It also directly affects female physiology and pathology.

Penetrating Vessel

Belt Vessel

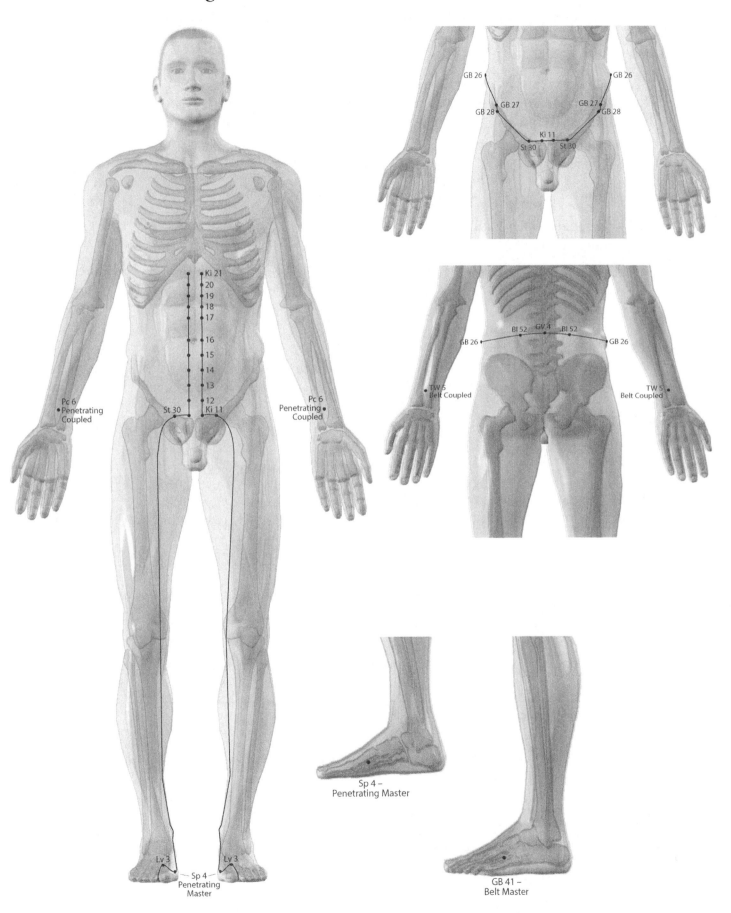

Ki 21
20
19
18
17
16
15
14
13
12
Ki 11

St 30

Pc 6
Penetrating
Coupled

Pc 6
Penetrating
Coupled

Lv 3

Lv 3

Sp 4 –
Penetrating
Master

GB 26

GB 27

GB 28

St 30

Ki 11

St 30

GB 26

GB 27

GB 28

Bl 52

GV 4

Bl 52

GB 26

GB 26

TW 5
Belt Coupled

TW 5
Belt Coupled

Sp 4 –
Penetrating Master

GB 41 –
Belt Master

Penetrating & Belt Vessels

Master Point:

Sp 4 公孫 Gongsun "Grandfather Grandson" (Lo Point)

Trace along the inferior aspect (underside) of the shaft of the metatarsal toward the heel to where the shaft meets the proximal head. Pressing into shaft, head and inferiorly into tissue.

Abdominal Swelling, Anorexia, Edema (Head), Epilepsy, Heart Inflammation, Hemorrhoids, Intestinal Hemorrhage, Pleurisy, Stomach Cancer, Vomiting.

Coupled Point:

Pc 6 內關 Neiguan "Inner Pass"

4 fingers superior to Pc 7 at the center of the wrist crease.

Emotional Problems, Menstrual Irregularity, Psychological Problems, Elbow Pain, Endocarditis, Eye Hemorrhage, Hiccups, Jaundice, Myocarditis, Stomach Pain.

Points:

Lv 3 太沖 Taichong "Supreme Rush"

On the top of the foot, the most proximal end of the space between the 1st and 2nd metatarsals.

Lumbar Pain, Mucous Discharge, Uterine Hemorrhage.

St 30 氣沖 Qichong "Qi Surge"

Just superior to the lateral corner of the pubic bone.

Abdominal Pain, All Genital Problems, Hernia, Impotency, Lumbago.

Ki 11 橫骨 Henggu "Pubic Bone"

On the superior edge of the pubic bone, halfway between the center (pubic symphysis) and lateral corner.

Eye Congestion or Inflammation, Hernia, Male Sterility, Mucous Discharge, Semen Leakage.

Ki 12-21 are each 2 fingers from the median line; 3 fingers between the left and right.

Ki 12 大赫 Dahe "Big Plentifulness"

3 fingers superior to Ki 11.

Eye Congestion or Inflammation, Male Sterility, Penis Pain, Sperm Insufficient, Vaginal Infection (Chronic).

Ki 13 氣穴 Qixue "Kidney Qi Cave"

3 fingers superior to Ki 12.

Back Pain or Spasm, Eye Congestion or Inflammation, Kidney Inflammation, Male Sterility, Semen Leakage.

Ki 14 四滿 Siman "Fourth for Fullnesses"

3 fingers superior to Ki 13.

Hernia, Intestinal Inflammation, Uterine Spasm, Vision Obscured.

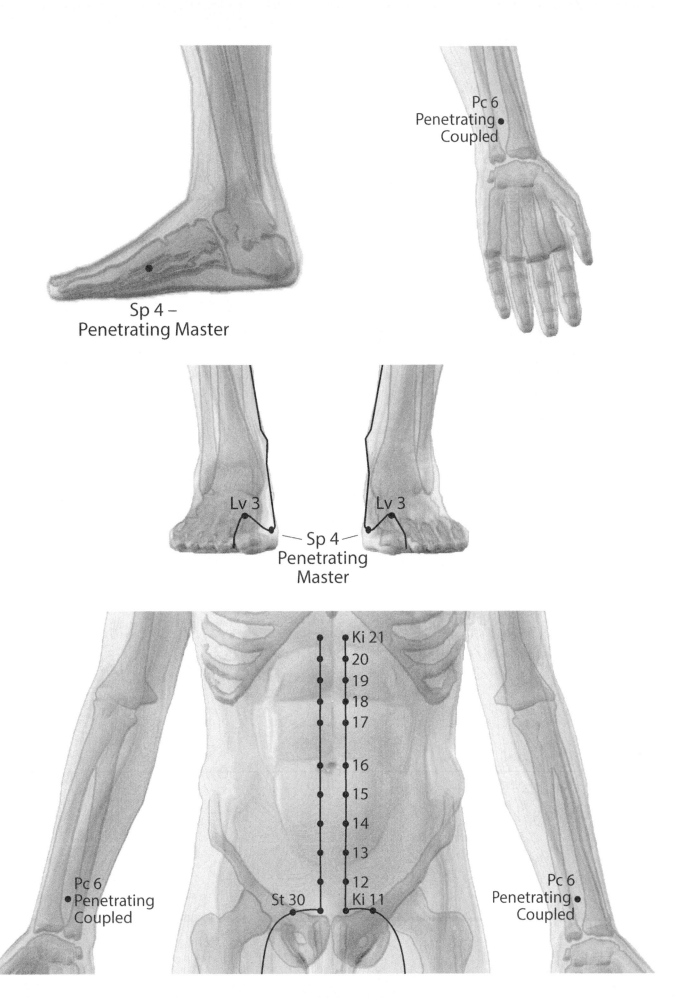

Sp 4 –
Penetrating Master

Pc 6
Penetrating
Coupled

Lv 3

Lv 3

— Sp 4 —
Penetrating
Master

Pc 6
Penetrating
Coupled

Pc 6
Penetrating
Coupled

Ki 21
20
19
18
17
16
15
14
13
12
Ki 11

St 30

Ki 15 中注 Zhongzhu "Pouring into the Middle"

3 fingers superior to Ki 14.

Constipation, Eustachian Tube Inflammation, Eye Congestion or Inflammation, Fallopian Inflammation, Intestinal Inflammation, Period Painful.

Ki 16 肓俞 Huangshu "Vitals Tissues Shu"

3 fingers outside of navel, 2 fingers superior to Ki 15.

Constipation (Chronic), Diarrhea, Eye Congestion or Inflammation, Hernia, Jaundice.

Ki 17 商曲 Shangqu "Metal Bend"

4 fingers superior to Ki 16.

Anorexia, Eye Congestion or Inflammation, Hernia, Jaundice.

Ki 18 石關 Shiguan "Stone Gate"

3 fingers superior to Ki 17.

Anorexia, Constipation, Eye Congestion, Mucous Discharge, Salivation Excessive, Uterine Congestion, Uterine Spasm.

Ki 19 陰都 Yindu "Yin Metropolis"

3 fingers superior to Ki 18.

Breathing Difficulty, Eye Congestion, Flatulence, Hernia, Pulmonary Emphysema, Vision Problems.

Ki 20 腹通谷 Futonggu "Abdominal Food Passage"

3 fingers superior to Ki 19.

Breathing Difficulty, Digestion Poor, Eye Congestion, Stomach Inflamed, Pulmonary Emphysema, Weakness.

Ki 21 幽門 Youmen "Hidden Gate"

3 fingers superior to Ki 20, just below the rib cage in the niche where the 6th and 7th ribs meet. The most superior you can fit 3 fingers laterally.

Bronchitis, Liver Problems, Morning Sickness, Swallowing Painful.

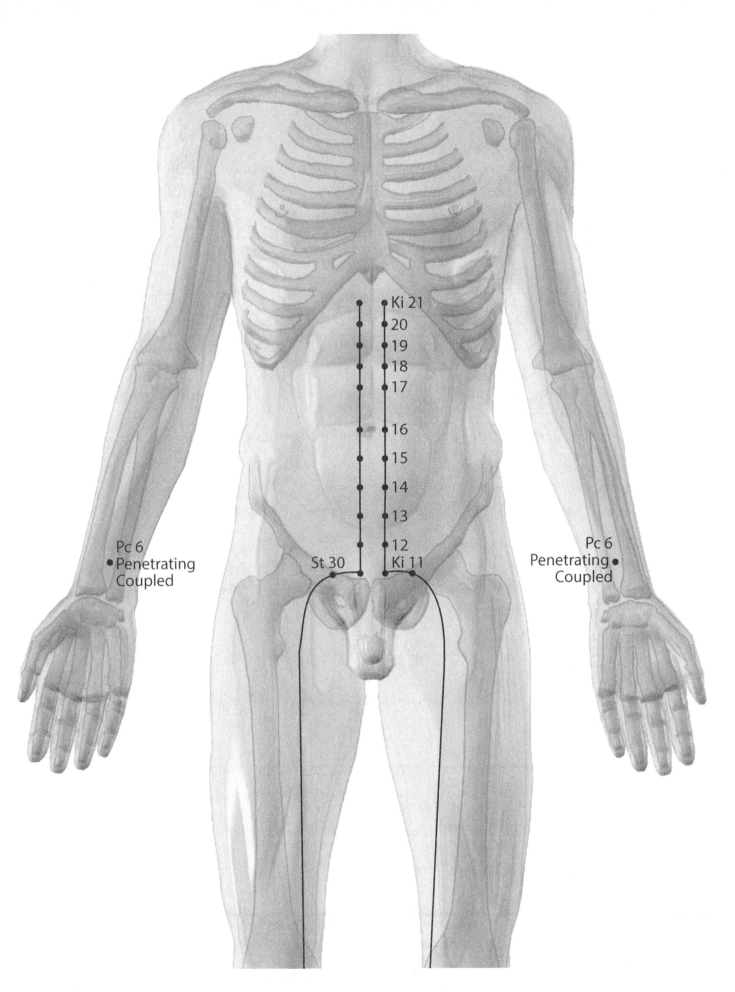

Ki 21
20
19
18
17
16
15
14
13
12
St 30   Ki 11

Pc 6
Penetrating
Coupled

Pc 6
Penetrating
Coupled

Belt Vessel Point Index

Master Point:

GB 41 足臨泣 Zulinqi "Foot Governor of Tears"

On the top of the foot, the most proximal end of the space between the 4th and 5th metatarsals.

All Skin Diseases, Pain, Breathing Problems, Breast Inflammation, Dizziness, Endocarditis, Fever, Headache, Periods Painful, Scrofula.

Coupled Point:

TW 5 外關 Waiguan "Outer Pass"

4 fingers proximal to the middle of the crease of the wrist, between the radius and the ulna.

Arthritis (Arm), Deafness, Eye Problems, Toothache.

Points:

Ki 11 橫骨 Henggu "Pubic Bone"

On the superior edge of the pubic bone, halfway between the center (pubic symphysis) and superior angle of the bone.

Eye Congestion or Inflammation, Hernia, Male Sterility, Mucous Discharge, Semen Leakage.

St 30 氣沖 Qichong "Qi Surge"

Just superior to the outside corner of the pubic bone.

Abdominal Pain, All Genital Problems, Hernia, Impotency, Lumbago.

GB 28 維道 Weidao "Linking Path"

Inferiorly 2 fingers from GB 27.

Abdominal Swelling, Anorexia, Cecum Inflamed, Colitis, Kidney Inflammation, Testicle Inflammation, Uterine Problems, Womb Inflammation.

GB 27 五樞 Wushu "Five Pivots"

2 fingers medialy from the ASIS (anterior superior iliac spine, the point at the top front of the hip bone).

Constipation, Hernia, Testicle Inflammation, Urinary Problems, Uterine Pain, Womb Inflammation.

GB 26 帶脈 Daimai "Girdling Vessel"

On the side of the body halfway between the ileum and the ribcage (11th rib).

Fever (From Cold), Periods Painful, Uterine Pain, Womb Inflammation.

Bl 52 志室 Zhishi "Willpower Room"

5 fingers laterally from GV 4.

Anuria, Bladder Infection, Cramp, Constipation.

GV 4 命門 Mingmen "Life Gate"

Between the spinous processes of L2 & 3—at the same level as Bl 23 the Ki Shu point..

Deafness, Ears Ring, Headache, Hemorrhoids, Hernia, Insomnia, Meningitis, Semen Leakage, Skin Dry, Urinary Incontinence, Vaginal Discharge.

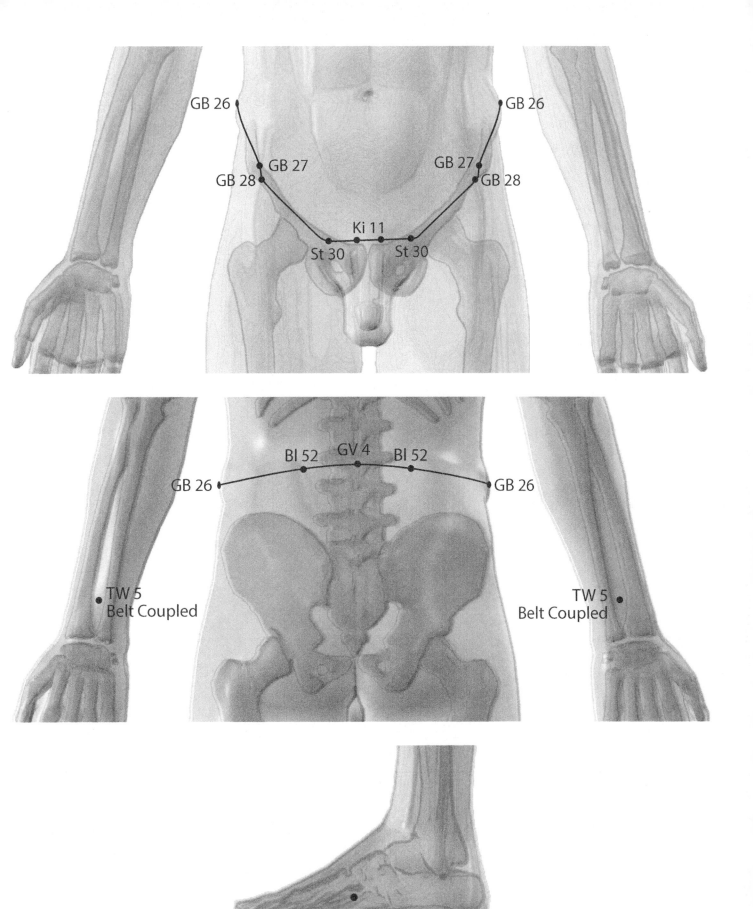

GB 26

GB 26

GB 27

GB 28

GB 27

GB 28

Ki 11

St 30

St 30

Bl 52

GV 4

Bl 52

GB 26

GB 26

TW 5
Belt Coupled

TW 5
Belt Coupled

GB 41 –
Belt Master

Penetrating & Belt Vessels

Index

A

D

E

Endocrine Glands 50
Endocrine System 2, 77
Enterocolitis 24, 32, 110, 112, 118, 120, 128
Epigastric Pain 102
Epilepsy 20, 24, 29, 38, 41, 42, 47, 48, 50, 57, 58, 63, 64, 74, 78, 80, 84, 86, 92, 108, 112, 114, 118, 120, 122, 126, 130, 132, 138, 142, 144, 148
Erection Involuntary 64, 138, 142
Esophagus Contraction 32
Esophagus Problems 8, 11
Esophagus Spasm 112, 114, 128, 140
Eustachian Tube Inflammation 66, 150
Excessive Dreaming 36
Excessive Laughter 36, 72
Excessive Mucus 6
Excessive Thinking 136, 146
Expressionless 36
Extra Meridians v, 1, 4, 106, 107, 116
Extraordinary Meridians iii, v, 1, 106, 107
Extremities Cold 116, 146
Eye Congestion 24, 42, 66, 80, 122, 148, 150, 152
Eye Congestion or Inflammation 66, 148, 150, 152
Eye Hemorrhage 74, 126, 148
Eyelid Spasm 17, 142
Eye Muscle Problems 17, 18, 84, 122, 142
Eye Problems 17, 24, 47, 50, 77, 78, 80, 83, 84, 92, 116, 120, 122, 130, 142, 152
Eyes Excess Tears 47
Eyesight Deterioration 118
Eyesight Poor 83
Eyesight Problems 74
Eyes Itch 122
Eyes Sore 40, 136
Eyes Sore, Red 40
Eyes Water Excessively 86, 130
Eyes Yellow 82

F

Face Red 72
Facial Abscess 17, 142
Facial Congestion 42, 84
Facial Spasms 83
Fainting 122
Fallopian Inflammation 66, 150
Fatigue 12, 24, 50, 64, 78, 136, 138, 142, 146
Fatigue in Limbs 50, 64, 138, 142
Fear 9, 14, 29, 30, 42, 46, 62, 136, 146
Fear of Abandonment 136, 146
Feeling and Expressing Emotions Difficult 72

Intercostal Pain 38, 39, 74
Internal Bleeding 50
Intestinal Hemorrhage 29, 32, 110, 118, 126, 128, 148
Intestinal Mucous 20
Intestinal Problems 50, 110
Intestinal Spasm 22

J

Jaundice 11, 20, 30, 48, 50, 63, 64, 66, 74, 88, 98, 102, 118, 120, 122, 126, 128, 132, 148, 150
Jaw Inflamed 44, 80
Jaw Inflammation 42, 120
Jaw Tension 16
Jealousy 46
Joint Pain 48, 136
Joint Stiffness 82
Jue 2, 72, 96
Junction Point 3

K

Kidney iii, 1, 2, 10, 20, 22, 46, 47, 50, 52, 56, 62, 63, 64, 66, 78, 88, 92, 97, 102, 108, 110, 112, 128, 132, 136, 144, 146, 148, 152
Kidney & Genital Inflammation 22
Kidney Inflammation 20, 22, 50, 52, 66, 78, 88, 92, 102, 110, 112, 128, 132, 144, 148, 152
Kidney Problems 56, 64, 136
Knee Arthritis 48, 58, 64, 144
Knee Pain 16, 28, 90
Knee Pain, Swelling 16
Knees Cold 22
Knee Swelling and Pain 22

L

Labor Difficult 59
Lack of Boundaries 6
Lack of Energy 62
Lack of Joy 36
Lack of Vitality 136
Lack of Will 82
Lactation Insufficient 32, 41, 74
Large Intestine iii, 1, 2, 3, 6, 7, 10, 11, 52, 62, 136
Large Intestine Meridian iii, 7, 10, 11
Laryngitis 11, 14, 18, 108
Lateral Paralysis 8, 12, 14, 132
Laziness 56
Leg & Foot Problems 146
Leg Pain 56, 100
Legs Cold 29, 98
Leg Spasm 90, 134

M

N

O

R

S

V

Vaginal Discharge 22, 30, 38, 88, 102, 118, 132, 144, 152
Vaginal Infection 48, 64, 66, 148
Vaginal Itch 38, 64, 138
Vaginal Pain 100
Vaginitis 30, 126
Vascular Problems 48
Vertigo 8, 9
Vision Blurred 72
Vision Obscured 41, 47, 66, 148
Vision Weakening 42, 44
Voice Loss 6
Voice Problems 18, 140
Vomiting 8, 14, 16, 18, 20, 24, 28, 29, 30, 38, 41, 42, 74, 78, 80, 102, 110, 112, 114, 118, 120, 122, 126, 128, 140, 148
Vomiting Blood 14, 20, 38, 41, 74, 110
Vomiting Mother's Milk (Babies) 112, 114

W

Waist Sore 146
Water Retention 8, 50, 56, 80, 112
Weakness 8, 18, 22, 24, 39, 50, 54, 66, 84, 88, 102, 110, 112, 120, 124, 132, 142, 150
Wei iii, 77, 106, 107, 124, 126, 130
Wei Mai iii, 106, 107, 124, 126, 130
Wei Qi 77, 106, 124
Well 3, 6, 9, 10, 16, 28, 36, 40, 46, 62, 63, 72, 76, 78, 82, 88, 96, 132, 142
Whooping Cough 18, 48
Womb Inflammation 20, 22, 30, 32, 38, 74, 88, 98, 110, 126, 152
Wood 1, 3, 6, 9, 10, 11, 16, 28, 36, 40, 46, 62, 72, 76, 82, 96
Wood point 3, 9, 11

Y

Yang vi, 1, 2, 3, 6, 10, 11, 12, 16, 24, 28, 36, 40, 42, 46, 47, 48, 54, 58, 62, 63, 72, 76, 77, 78, 82, 84, 90, 92, 106, 107, 108, 116, 118, 124, 130, 134, 136, 142, 144, 146
Yang Meridian 106
Yang Qiao Mai 106, 107, 136, 142, 146
Yang Wei Mai 106, 107, 124, 130
Yawning 16
Yin vi, 1, 2, 3, 6, 10, 16, 22, 28, 30, 36, 38, 40, 46, 59, 62, 63, 64, 66, 72, 82, 84, 92, 96, 100, 102, 106, 107, 108, 110, 124, 126, 136, 138, 146, 150
Yin Meridian 106
Yin Qiao Mai 106, 107, 136, 138, 146
Yin Wei Mai 106, 107, 124, 126
Yin/Yang 3
Yuan Points 3
Yuan Qi 146

Printed in Great Britain
by Amazon

47575244R00097